THE UNREASONABLE

OTHERWORLDLY. UNCOMPROMISING. DIVINE.

COLLIN LEE

Jesus the Unreasonable

ISBN: 978-1-958723-84-5.

Cover design: Roy Appalsamy of Toronto, Ontario. Interior layout: Toney C. Mulhollan.

Illumination Publishers titles may be purchased in bulk for classroom instruction, business, fundraising, or sales promotional use. For information, please email toneyipibooks@mac.com. We care deeply about using renewable resources and use recycled paper whenever possible.

About the author: **Collin Lee** is a graduate of the University of Southern California who served in the fulltime ministry in Los Angeles before starting a marketing career that spans more than 25 years. He also served as the first elder of his local congregation in Santa Clarita, California, where he continues to preach and teach alongside the church leadership. He is an experienced copywriter and the author of a National Gold IPPY Award-winning picture book *The Efil Brothers.* His recent book, *The Prodigal Son: A Poetic Journey,* was published by Theatron Press.

Contents

Preface

Why another book about Jesus?

I had to write this one for myself. Here is my confession. After having lived more than three and a half decades as a born-again Christian and served my church in various ways, including as a full-time minister and an elder, I was...tired, not only physically but also emotionally, and more than anything, spiritually. I felt like I wanted to simply press the cruise control button on my spiritual steering wheel and coast my way into heaven. It was not that I felt my labor in Christ was in vain, it was just that the ministerial challenges in my life have worn me out. I am quite confident that many of you feel the same, whether you are a veteran Christian or a newbie. I have been feeling this gnawing sense of complacency in our churches in my spirit. Through my many conversations with brothers and sisters in our local church and beyond, it was clear to me that this spiritual fatigue that I was experiencing was more than personal; it was universal.

So I knew what I had to do: Go back to God's word, specifically Jesus' teaching, where my humble faith began. And once I was into those red letters in the Bible, I was reminded of who my Lord and Savior is:

Jesus *the Unreasonable.*

What He taught was more than radical. When something is radical, it is still within the realm of humanity, but His teaching was from above, otherworldly, unreasonable...with a divine purpose. He set the tone of His entire ministry early on during the famous Sermon on the Mount. He turned the then-current theology upside down with this series of teachings, and in the middle of it is this profound statement:

> *"Therefore you are to be perfect, as your heavenly Father is perfect."*
>
> —Matthew 5:48

Be perfect? Really? We all know that what He was teaching was not the perfectionism that we are familiar with. It was much deeper than that, more fundamental. He was leading His followers on a spiritual journey *toward* perfection, not one of *becoming* perfection, hence it would be a lifelong pursuit of holiness.

Our spiritual goal has to be a constantly moving target, out of our reach every time. This is not to frustrate us or make us feel hopeless. It is to prevent us from being complacent in our spiritual walk, regardless of how long we have been Jesus' followers. He is pushing us to push ourselves. Better yet, in His own words, to *deny* ourselves.

Jesus' teaching had to be unreasonable so that we could not reason ourselves out of it, but would strive and labor to listen and obey, not in our own strength, but in the power of the Spirit that is within us. This is hard, very hard. And in this striving and laboring, we become tired. Yet the divine irony is this: The journey of striving to obey His word often pushes us against a spiritual wall, but dwelling in His same word in turn empowers us to break through it.

So here I go, wrestling with the unreasonableness of His teaching, so that I can experience the divine strength that Paul experienced:

> *And He has said to me, "My grace is sufficient for you, for power is perfected in weakness." Most gladly, therefore, I will rather boast about my weaknesses, so that the power of Christ may dwell in me. Therefore I am well content with weaknesses, with insults, with distresses, with persecutions, with difficulties, for Christ's sake; for when I am weak, then I am strong.*
>
> —2 Corinthians 12:9–10

Yes, His *unreasonable* teaching will reveal our weaknesses. But unlike how the world sees it, it will be a blessing, not a detriment. It will be a spiritual breath of fresh air for those of us who are tired.

May we wholeheartedly embrace our Lord and Savior as who He really is:

Jesus the Unreasonable.

In Him,

Collin Lee

Chapter One

Unreasonable Forgiveness

Forgiving is not natural. As someone who has struggled with the sin of outbursts of anger, I can definitely tell you that it is not natural. What is natural is this: Newton's third law of motion, which states, *for every action, there is an equal and opposite reaction.* In other words, when someone hurts you, you hurt back. Now, that *feels* right.

Another thing about forgiving is that everyone has a threshold. We tend to think that we are more forgiving than we really are. We go on forgiving those little offenses in our lives until we find ourselves outraged by something, usually something unexpected, so we were unable to prepare for it. We react, rather than respond. We let our emotions get the best of us instead of the spiritually trained mindset of forgiving.

So we understand that the heart of forgiving is

attained, not innate. We need to learn the truth about forgiving and being forgiven from Jesus Himself, and the following scripture is a good start:

> *Then Peter came and said to Him, "Lord, how often shall my brother sin against me and I forgive him? Up to seven times?" Jesus said to him, "I do not say to you, up to seven times, but up to seventy times seven.*
>
> *"For this reason the kingdom of heaven may be compared to a king who wished to settle accounts with his slaves. When he had begun to settle them, one who owed him ten thousand talents was brought to him. But since he did not have the means to repay, his lord commanded him to be sold, along with his wife and children and all that he had, and repayment to be made. So the slave fell to the ground and prostrated himself before him, saying, 'Have patience with me and I will repay you everything.' And the lord of that slave felt compassion and released him and forgave him the debt. But that slave went out and found one of his fellow slaves who owed him a hundred denarii; and he seized him and began to choke him, saying, 'Pay back what you owe.' So his fellow slave fell to the ground and began to plead with him, saying, 'Have patience with me and I will repay you.' But he was unwilling and went and threw him in prison until he should pay back what was owed. So when his fellow slaves saw what had happened, they were deeply grieved and came and reported to their lord all that had happened. Then summoning him, his lord said to him, 'You wicked slave, I forgave you all that debt because you pleaded with me. Should you not also have had mercy on your fellow slave, in the same way that I had mercy on you?' And his lord, moved with anger, handed him over to the torturers until he should repay all that was owed*

him. My heavenly Father will also do the same to you, if each of you does not forgive his brother from your heart."

—Matthew 18:21–35

Peter was just like us. He wanted his teacher's affirmation that he was a forgiving person, full of grace and mercy. I can just imagine him confidently saying, "Up to seven times?" But Jesus' response was, yes, unreasonable.

Being a Jew himself, Peter likely understood the significance of "seventy times seven," a numerological representation of perfection in the Jewish culture. Jesus was saying that Peter's forgiving should be of perfection, that is, forgive always, without limits. I wonder what Peter's expression was like as he listened to this absurd answer to what he most likely thought was a rhetorical question.

But Jesus did not stop at this unreasonableness. He continued with a lesson on forgiveness through a parable that was also utterly unreasonable when you consider the amounts of money that were involved.

During Jesus' days, a denarius was the typical daily wage of a common laborer. So a hundred denarii would be about three to four months of work. It was a significant amount of money, but still payable. This was the amount that a fellow slave owed our antagonistic slave.

Now the kicker is this: When we consider what the main-character slave owed his master in denarii, the comparison becomes dramatic. The numbers become unreasonable. One talent was worth about 6,000 denarii, and he owed 10,000 talents, which would have been an astounding 60,000,000 denarii! That was 200,000 years of labor! Let me put this in our modern-day perspective: The main-character slave was forgiven $9,600,000,000 of debt by his master, but he couldn't forgive his fellow slave's $16,000 debt!

Jesus wanted Peter and other disciples to know where the motivation for the seventy times seven was to come from: God's abundant—shall we say, unreasonable?—forgiveness of their own sins. The hard fact is that, for every single one of us with no exceptions, we have more to be forgiven than to forgive on a daily basis. In our own eyes, we may be pretty good people, but from God's perspective, we are utterly and completely sinful.

And this is where the world tries to deceive us. We often hear people say, "God loves us just the way we are." It surely sounds good, but it is not true at all. It is not the gospel we find in the Bible.

God loves us, not just the way we are, but despite *who we are.*

Yes, God loves all of us, but He sent His Son Jesus

to die on the cross for us so that we would have an opportunity to follow Jesus, learn from Him and eventually become like Him, not remain as ourselves. If God loves us just the way we are, why would He pave the most sacrificial way for us to transform into someone completely different from ourselves spiritually, namely Jesus Christ? The world wants us to focus only on ourselves, to make ourselves feel good. It is all about *self*: self-confidence, self-esteem, self-reliance, self-love—you name it.

"If it feels right, it must be right."

"Let no one tell you that you are not good enough."

"Believe in yourself."

"Trust your heart."

"Love yourself."

These all sound inspirational, don't they? But these are not biblical principles. I know what some of you are thinking: *"Loving yourself is biblical, since there are several scriptures about loving your neighbor as yourself."* But if you look at these scriptures closely, you will notice something that you may not have seen before. Let's take one of them and examine it:

> *And He said to him, "'YOU SHALL LOVE THE LORD YOUR GOD WITH ALL YOUR HEART, AND WITH ALL YOUR SOUL, AND WITH ALL YOUR MIND.' This is the great and foremost commandment. The second is like*

> *it, 'YOU SHALL LOVE YOUR NEIGHBOR AS YOURSELF.' On these two commandments depend the whole Law and the Prophets."*
>
> —Matthew 22:37–40

Even structurally, this statement does not say, "Love God. Love neighbor. Love yourself." Rather, it is basically saying, "Love God. Love your neighbor as yourself." Hence the word "as" plays a critical role in understanding this teaching. It is ώς (*hos*) in Greek, and contextually, it is most accurately translated as "in the same manner as" or "after the fashion of." So Jesus here was not commanding us to love ourselves, but simply acknowledging that we love ourselves anyway. He was commanding us to love those around us in the same manner as we naturally love ourselves. So the proper twist to this scripture would be: Love your neighbor, *not just* yourself. This, then, aligns correctly with His other teachings about denying oneself, taking up one's cross, and dying to oneself daily.

I have realized that whenever I train my mind to accept the fact that I do not deserve anything good on my own—that is, at least doing my best to embrace the truth that I am a hopeless sinner without God's love, grace and mercy—it is much easier for me to forgive someone. What I need is not any of those self-somethings but only the self-awareness of who I really am in God's eyes: a redeemed sinner through the blood of Jesus on the cross. A sinner nonetheless.

His teaching could not be any clearer: God forgave you more than you could ever know and continues to forgive you every day through thick and thin. So forgive those around you unconditionally. Otherwise, you will be judged accordingly.

But the challenge remains. How are we to forgive unconditionally? As I mentioned in my introduction, if we have the right perspective on this call for perfection, His intention with this teaching will be clear. This scripture demonstrates the idea adequately:

> *And someone said to Him, "Lord, are there just a few who are being saved?" And He said to them, "Strive to enter through the narrow door; for many, I tell you, will seek to enter and will not be able."*
>
> —Luke 13:23–24

The word "strive" here in acient Greek is ἀγωνίζομαι (*agonizomai*), which means "to struggle, like engaged in an intense athletic contest or warfare," and as you surely guessed, our English word "agonize" comes from this word. When Jesus was asked about being saved, He taught this person that basically one should fight like crazy to enter through the narrow door. Our Christian life is destined to be a struggle, and not just any struggle, but something that we would agonize over. (Sorry for being a party pooper for those who believe that Christianity is a feel-good religion.)

So in forgiving others, we should take the same attitude: Struggle and fight like never before to forgive. Whatever gets in the way of our forgiving, we cannot minimize, dismiss, or excuse it; instead, we have to do all we can to forgive. Despite all this, when—not if but when—we fail to forgive, we still learn something: that we are indeed weak on our own. This consequently motivates us that much more to desperately seek His power that is within us, however difficult it may be. And this is what we signed up for when we became Jesus' followers. Remember, following is not just about believing but also about living, which includes both spiritual victories and defeats.

For the world, however, the fight is not about forgiving, it is about justice. More than ever, people are demanding justice in many different ways. Of course, justice itself is not wrong. God is just. But if the call for justice becomes a facade for revenge, the consequence is dire for all of us, since we know that revenge begets revenge.

In our current world that seems to sit on a powder keg, forgiveness (forgiving and being forgiven) is the only hope, but ironically it is seen as a weakness, so only a few want to embrace it. Forgiveness is the only way to break the cycle of hate, but we are too wrapped up in ourselves—our wants, needs, and rights—to be able to see it clearly. And what we are talking about here are not those little sorries that we quickly respond to with "No worries." It is the kind of forgiveness that can only come from gut-wrenching self-denial, a truly spiritual response to the most heinous offense. It is the unreasonable forgiveness that Jesus is calling us to learn and obey.

But why such a high calling for forgiving, especially for His followers? It is because He knows us too well. He knows that forgiving helps heal the forgiver more than the forgiven, and it transforms the heart and mind of the forgiver to maturity in Christ. By forgiving, we become that much more like Jesus.

A tired soul like me, however, often has a hard time forgiving, having seen an act of forgiveness misunderstood and mistreated time and again. Time wears on, and one feels indifferent or cynical about the power of forgiveness. The world makes one's forgiving look like waving a white flag. I have been there. I felt like my attempt to be like Jesus in forgiving was not making an ounce of difference in the difficult situation that I was in. At times, I felt like I was treated like the offender instead of the offended. I was discouraged, distraught, hurt, and even raging inside. So, as a last resort, although it should have been the first resort, I knew where I needed to go: the cross.

> *When they came to the place called The Skull, there they crucified Him and the criminals, one on the right and the other on the left. But Jesus was saying, "Father, forgive them; for they do not know what they are doing." And they cast lots, dividing up His garments among themselves.*
>
> —Luke 23:33–34

The Gospels mention only seven utterances of Jesus while He was on the cross, and this particular one has the most remarkable—more aptly described as unreasonable—words of forgiving! Whenever I come across this scripture, my response is the same…a silence of awe. There can be no words to describe someone who is forgiving those who are killing him in the most excruciating way possible at that time. The very word "excruciating" even comes from the punishment of crucifixion and how inhumane it was.

There He was, stripped naked, nailed to the cross, and gasping for air while in physical shock with the kind of pain that the human body was not meant to bear. And He had to go through it all alone. Not even the heavenly Father was there. He was completely forsaken by all. Yet He fought and agonized to keep the heart to forgive His executioners, not in retrospect but in real time as He was actually going through the crucifixion. How? No words, simply no words.

So with this Jesus on the cross in front of us, forgive, we must. And the real forgiving comes from the heart, which means we have no choice but to dig deep within us to be able to forgive in a way that is even remotely like our Lord and Savior, Jesus the *Unreasonable.*

Chapter Two

Unreasonable Devotion

> *Now large crowds were going along with Him; and He turned and said to them, "If anyone comes to Me, and does not hate his own father and mother and wife and children and brothers and sisters, yes, and even his own life, he cannot be My disciple."*
>
> —Luke 14:25–26

In my experience of studying the Bible with hundreds of people, this particular scripture puzzled many of them because of the word "hate." To them, the word just did not match who Jesus was, a teacher who taught people to love even their enemies. Did He really mean what He said?

The word "hate" in Greek is μισέω (*miseo*), which means "to detest on a comparative basis," and everything starts to make sense when we look at the parallel scripture in Matthew:

"He who loves father or mother more than Me is not worthy of Me; and he who loves son or daughter more than Me is not worthy of Me."

—Matthew 10:37

Jesus taught His followers to love Him more than anyone, even more than one's own family, so in comparison, it would even seem like hate. Now this is hard teaching! It is especially hard emotionally when you consider that our families are flesh and blood while Jesus is the Word with whom we can only connect spiritually. Loving our families whom we can see and live with is naturally much easier than loving Jesus, who only lives in our hearts and minds. Yet His call for the ultimate devotion to Him is not an option; it is an essential condition of following Him, becoming His disciple, a Christian, which literally means a "small Christ."

If we consider Jesus as just a good teacher or a good religious leader, this command sounds absurd. We have seen enough examples of cults of personality in the media to know that this kind of call for loyalty and devotion is dangerous and destructive. Instead of being devoted, one can become fanatical toward the leader. We should remember that devotion is a virtue, characterized by sincere love and loyalty, while fanaticism is a vice, marked by extreme, uncritical, and often harmful adherence to a belief or cause. The motivation behind devotion is selfless, while selfish ambition or desire drives fanaticism.

Jesus was not just a good teacher or a good religious leader. He did not start a new belief or religion. He started *the way to a new life*. He was not just somebody; He was the Word from which the entire universe came into existence (John 1:3). He was, and is, and will always be *the Creator*. He created all of us and all of our families. With this understanding, His command for the ultimate devotion to Him sounds different. It makes sense. The Creator is commanding His creations to have the closest relationship possible with Him, so that His creations can experience the fullness of what it means to be with Him.

So what does loving Jesus more than our families look like? This is what it looked like to Him:

> *Then His mother and His brothers arrived, and standing outside they sent word to Him and called Him. A crowd was sitting around Him, and they said to Him, "Behold, Your mother and Your brothers are outside looking for You." Answering them, He said, "Who are My mother and My brothers?" Looking about at those who were sitting around Him, He said, "Behold My mother and My brothers! For whoever does the will of God, he is My brother and sister and mother."*
>
> —Mark 3:31–35

Earlier in the chapter (Mark 3:20–21), we read that Jesus' family went to take charge of Him because they thought that He was out of His mind. By this time, we can see from the Gospels that His father Joseph most likely had passed away, which means as the firstborn of the family, He should have been taking care of the family business of carpentry. Instead, He was completely immersed in His ministry. No wonder His family was compelled to intervene. His family needed Him. But Jesus' response to their visit was clear and resolute. To Him, the most important agenda of the day was doing the will of God, in other words, obeying God's word. He did not say that His family was not important, but He made sure everyone knew what mattered to Him the most, the ultimate purpose of His life, which was all about obeying His Father in Heaven. As a matter of fact, in the verses right before Matthew 10:37, which I mentioned previously, Jesus was even more graphic about the cost of this kind of devotion:

> *"Do not think that I came to bring peace on the earth; I did not come to bring peace, but a sword. For I came to SET A MAN AGAINST HIS FATHER, AND A DAUGHTER AGAINST HER MOTHER, AND A DAUGHTER-IN-LAW AGAINST HER MOTHER-IN-LAW; and A MAN'S ENEMIES WILL BE THE MEMBERS OF HIS HOUSEHOLD."*
>
> —Matthew 10:34–36

For some, this is not a hyperbole but a reality, having to persevere through persecutions from their own families just because they made the decision to follow Jesus. Going to church is one thing, but becoming a disciple of Jesus means having a renewed mind, heart, and lifestyle, which can sometimes be misunderstood or downright opposed. Nevertheless, Jesus wants them to stand firm on their devotion to Him, not just in their thoughts, but also in their deeds:

> *And He was saying to them all, "If anyone wishes to come after Me, he must deny himself, and take up his cross daily and follow Me. For whoever wishes to save his life will lose it, but whoever loses his life for My sake, he is the one who will save it."*
>
> —Luke 9:23–24

This is a scripture that many of us know by heart, but this cost of the discipleship of Jesus is not readily preached in churches nowadays. "It's so old school," some say. But the fact is that Christianity *is* old. The better way to put it is that Christianity is *timeless*. People want to feel loved, comforted, encouraged, and uplifted in the church. True, these desires in themselves are not bad, but the ultimate goal of our worship and fellowship should not be focused on ourselves and meeting our own needs. It should be all about God, who He is and how He should be revered, honored, glorified, and loved by us. In multiple scriptures, we see that loving Him comes down to one thing: *obedience.*

> *"He who has My commandments and keeps them is the one who loves Me; and he who loves Me will be loved by My Father, and I will love him and will disclose Myself to him."*
>
> —John 14:21

> *Jesus answered and said to him, "If anyone loves Me, he will keep My word; and My Father will love him, and We will come to him and make Our abode with him."*
>
> —John 14:23

> *"If you keep My commandments, you will abide in My love; just as I have kept My Father's commandments and abide in His love."*
>
> —John 15:10

> *Whoever keeps His word, in him the love of God has truly been perfected. By this we know that we are in Him:*
>
> —1 John 2:5

It is notable how John, who was known as "the disciple whom Jesus loved" (John 21:20), was the one who taught that loving God means obeying His word. Having faith in Jesus is indeed pleasing to Him, but John shows us that there is more to it than that in our Christianity. Jesus expects us to *be* and *do* as His followers beyond simply believing. His call for unreasonable devotion is about obedience.

Again, within this unreasonableness, there is a deeper truth that governs our human relationships. There is a divine reason why putting Jesus first in our lives makes our relationships better, on an earthly level and a heavenly level:

> *And if one can overpower him who is alone, two can resist him. A cord of three strands is not quickly torn apart.*
>
> —Ecclesiastes 4:12

A common rope that we can buy at a nearby hardware store is usually three strands, and those strands indeed make the rope strong. You will be hard pressed to find one with two strands. As such, in a relationship between two individuals, having Jesus as the "third strand" indeed makes the relationship much stronger. Having His word as the common denominator of perspectives and expectations, people are able to come to a common understanding of a disputed matter, hence it is possible to resolve conflict. So putting Jesus above all else in a relationship actually makes the relationship stronger. And even if only one of the two individuals in a relationship puts Jesus above all else, that one's humility in Christ will go a long way in building a strong relationship between them, and perhaps the other one may be influenced spiritually and eventually seek and find God.

Beyond human relationships, there are many other things in our daily lives that compete with our ultimate devotion to Jesus. Our lives are supposedly automated more than ever before, but instead of having more time because of that, everyone seems to be chasing after time.

We are just too busy.

People say that it is quality over quantity when it comes to a good relationship, but the truth is that both quality and quantity are important if we are to have a truly meaningful relationship.

We need time.

And with Jesus, it is no different. We know those sporadic Bible readings and prayers are not enough to help us mature in Christ. We also know that having Jesus foremost in our thoughts throughout the day is challenging because many of the things that we need to take care of are not directly related to our Christianity, so we do not think about Jesus. These are usually urgent things to be done, and when they do not go the way we planned, out goes our spirituality. We get annoyed, irritated, frustrated, angry, and stressed out.

So how do we keep Jesus top of mind as we go about our crazy day? I tried different things in the past, and one practice seemed to work well, at least for me. It is nothing special, enigmatic, or miraculous. It is what many devoted followers of God used to practice for thousands of years. It is to recite:

The LORD is my shepherd,
I shall not want.
He makes me lie down in green pastures;
He leads me beside quiet waters.
He restores my soul;
He guides me in the paths of righteousness
For His name's sake.
Even though I walk through the valley of the shadow of death,
I fear no evil, for You are with me;
Your rod and Your staff, they comfort me.
You prepare a table before me in the presence of my enemies;
You have anointed my head with oil;
My cup overflows.
Surely goodness and lovingkindness will follow me
all the days of my life,
And I will dwell in the house of the LORD forever.

—Psalm 23

The above is the famous Psalm 23, widely known as the Shepherd's Psalm, and it has the universal theme of comfort and security. It is believed to have been recited by the British and German soldiers together during the famous Christmas Truce of 1914 during the First World War. It has the inexplicable power to bring peace that transcends all understanding to the hearer.

So what I do is memorize it and recite it throughout the day whenever possible, and it only takes a minute. Some may think it is repetitive and monotonous, but sometimes I find myself not even knowing what to pray, so borrowing King David's words helps me to focus on what really matters in my life, Jesus my Lord and Savior. I went on to pick up other psalms to memorize and recite, and I can definitely say that it has changed my spiritual life. The Psalms are rich in their diverse contexts, so it is easy to find just the right psalm depending on what one is going through. And I personalize all those "enemies" in the Psalms as the challenges in my life. Satan is real, and he opposes every one of God's children. It is imperative to recognize his schemes in our lives.

In addition to the Shepherd's Psalm, I decided to memorize and recite the following psalm because it helps me pour out my heart when I am discouraged. In a way, it is the right way to complain to God. I slowly recite it, meditating on each word. By the end of the psalm, somehow I usually find peace, and at other times at least a sense of a spiritual anchor grounding my emotions.

How long, O LORD Will You forget me forever?
How long will You hide Your face from me?
How long shall I take counsel in my soul,
Having sorrow in my heart all the day?
How long will my enemy be exalted over me?
Consider and answer me, O LORD my God;
Enlighten my eyes, or I will sleep the sleep of death,
And my enemy will say, "I have overcome him,"
And my adversaries will rejoice when I am shaken.
But I have trusted in Your lovingkindness;
My heart shall rejoice in Your salvation.
I will sing to the LORD,
Because He has dealt bountifully with me.

—Psalm 13

And the next psalm is for when my mind is filled with so many things that I feel overwhelmed. It is like a spiritual deep breath that I take to center myself in God.

O LORD, my heart is not proud, nor my eyes haughty;
Nor do I involve myself in great matters,
Or in things too difficult for me.
Surely I have composed and quieted my soul;
Like a weaned child rests against his mother,
My soul is like a weaned child within me.
O Israel, hope in the LORD
From this time forth and forever.

—Psalm 131

Our devotion to Jesus takes many shapes, but all in all, it requires giving all our hearts and minds to it, and how we do that is something we should continue to explore and learn throughout our lives. What used to work for us may not work now. What works now may not work in the future. It is a journey with many turns and forks in the road, and only one thing is required: that you keep going.

Last, Jesus' call for unreasonable devotion demands our acceptance of Him as both our Savior *and* Lord. Confessing Jesus as the Savior only requires one's repentance, but confessing Him as the Lord requires our surrender. As Lord, He owns every part of our lives, and we should live accordingly. Do we live our lives as we want or directed by His word? What do our daily lives look like to others? Can they tell that Jesus is our Lord, that He *owns* and *controls* our lives? Do they only see us as churchgoers or something much more? Do they see us making difficult decisions and being willing to pay the price just because those decisions are biblical? Do they see that we value the biblical truth above all else in our lives, even in defining what true love is?

It is easy to go to church, sing worship songs, pray, and be nice to others. It is easy to confess, "Jesus is my Savior," and even, "Jesus is Lord." But the kind of devotion that Jesus seeks is something that comes from wrestling within.

Devotion is what it is, not because it is easy, but because it is hard.

It is *unreasonable.*

Chapter Three

Unreasonable Inclusion

The Gospels recount time and again that Jesus reached out to those who were outcasts and marginalized—the tax collectors, lepers, prostitutes, demon possessed, sick, lame, blind, and crippled. But these acts of outreach across social barriers were not just to be nice to them and help them. There was an ultimate purpose:

> *"For the Son of Man has come to seek and to save that which was lost."*
>
> —Luke 19:10

He included all these people in His life because it was the only way for them to have the opportunity to know God and turn to Him. Jesus' purpose was not social but spiritual. Paul took on this same spirit of Jesus:

> *For though I am free from all men, I have made myself a slave to all, so that I may win more. To the Jews I became as a Jew, so that I might win Jews; to those who are under the Law, as under the Law though not being myself under the Law, so that I might win those who are under the Law; to those who are without law, as without law, though not being without the law of God but under the law of Christ, so that I might win those who are without law. To the weak I became weak, that I might win the weak; I have become all things to all men, so that I may by all means save some.*
>
> —1 Corinthians 9:19–22

The level of inclusion that God talks about through Paul is more than just being friendly. It is more important for those who are in our lives to feel like we are one of them than for them to feel like they are one of us. It obviously does not mean that we should condone people's sins or sinful lifestyles, but it does mean that we are invested in their lives, and that we are humble, gracious, and merciful toward them.

This goes against the grain of the world, where we are to make friends on our own terms. But again, Jesus' call for inclusion is unreasonable because our friendships are supposed to be solely based on serving and giving. The world says that a friendship should be reciprocal, but Jesus says that it should be sacrificial. The world offers friendships to those who are alike, who have common interests, goals, and dreams. But Jesus commands us to offer our friendships to *all* because it is not about us, but about them.

And Jesus did not just teach it, He lived it daily. The following story is the epitome of His unreasonable inclusion:

> *And He had to pass through Samaria. So He came to a city of Samaria called Sychar, near the parcel of ground that Jacob gave to his son Joseph; and Jacob's well was there. So Jesus, being wearied from His journey, was sitting thus by the well. It was about the sixth hour.*
>
> *There came a woman of Samaria to draw water. Jesus said to her, "Give Me a drink." For His disciples had gone away into the city to buy food. Therefore the Samaritan woman said to Him, "How is it that You, being a Jew, ask me for a drink since I am a Samaritan woman?" (For Jews have no dealings with Samaritans.) Jesus answered and said to her, "If you knew the gift of God, and who it is who says to you, 'Give Me a drink,' you would have asked Him, and He would have given you living water." She said to Him, "Sir, You have nothing to draw with and the well is deep; where then do You get that living water? You are not greater than our father Jacob, are You, who gave us the well, and drank of it himself and his sons and his cattle?" Jesus answered and said to her, "Everyone who drinks of this water will thirst again; but whoever drinks of the water*

that I will give him shall never thirst; but the water that I will give him will become in him a well of water springing up to eternal life."

The woman said to Him, "Sir, give me this water, so I will not be thirsty nor come all the way here to draw." He said to her, "Go, call your husband and come here." The woman answered and said, "I have no husband." Jesus said to her, "You have correctly said, 'I have no husband'; for you have had five husbands, and the one whom you now have is not your husband; this you have said truly." The woman said to Him, "Sir, I perceive that You are a prophet. Our fathers worshiped in this mountain, and you people say that in Jerusalem is the place where men ought to worship." Jesus said to her, "Woman, believe Me, an hour is coming when neither in this mountain nor in Jerusalem will you worship the Father. You worship what you do not know; we worship what we know, for salvation is from the Jews. But an hour is coming, and now is, when the true worshipers will worship the Father in spirit and truth; for such people the Father seeks to be His worshipers. God is spirit, and those who worship Him must worship in spirit and truth." The woman said to Him, "I know that Messiah is coming (He who is called Christ); when that One comes, He will declare all things to us." Jesus said to her, "I who speak to you am He."

—John 4:4–26

When we look at this famous story, we usually gloss over a phrase in verse 4, "And He *had to* pass through Samaria," but within it is a theological gem. The words "had to" in Greek are the word δει (*dei*), which means "absolutely necessary," and in this context, it literally means "necessity brought on by circumstances or by the conduct of others toward us." Typically for Jews at that time who were traveling from Judea to Galilee, they would pass through Perea and Decapolis to avoid Samaria, since Jews and Samaritans had deep-seated animosity and avoided interactions, considering each other ritually impure. But for Jesus, it was a divine plan that He had to meet this woman at the well of Sychar. It was absolutely necessary. The barriers for inclusion had to be broken in an unreasonable way.

The odds were stacked against this woman to meet and interact with Jesus. First of all, the time of day, about noon, was not typical for women to come and draw water from the well, but she was there, most likely to avoid meeting other women who might gossip about her. Second, she was a Samaritan, so for a Jew to start up a conversation with her would have been very unlikely. Third, she was a woman. It was improper for a man, especially a religious teacher, to speak with a woman alone in public, let alone a foreign woman. Fourth, being Jesus, He would have known her outcast social status because of her sinful marital situation. And last, Jesus did not stop at speaking to her but asked her for water, intending to use her vessel to drink, which would have been considered unclean.

All these barriers to inclusion were real, but Jesus

broke them all in broad daylight for the whole world to see. Jesus' example of unreasonable inclusion was loud and clear: *No one* is excluded.

At the same time, Jesus did not accept her sins. He confronted them with patience, grace, and mercy, so that she could repent. He also went on to teach her about worshiping God in spirit and truth. He did not stop at accepting and including her into His life; He set out to give her a new life. His inclusion had a divine purpose beyond simply building a relationship.

One of the ways to show a heart of inclusion is hospitality. During Jesus' day, hospitality was a common virtue. In a world without hotels, Airbnb, or widespread public transportation, travelers had to depend on the kindness of locals for water, food, and lodging. The word "hospitality" in Greek is φιλοξενία (*philoxenia*), which comes from φίλος (*philos*) and ξένος (*xenos*), which respectively mean "friends" and "strangers." So the word "hospitality" literally means "being a friend to strangers."

Two thousand years later in our modern society, the concept of hospitality has changed. It would be naive to think that we can simply welcome strangers into our homes. Unfortunately, the world is too dangerous for that. But we can still be hospitable by showing kindness to strangers in small and big ways, and we can certainly invite those we know to our homes to share meals and our lives together. The concept of hospitality may have changed because of the changes in our society, but the heart of hospitality is something we as Christians can carry on. But to do that, we should ask these important questions:

Who is in our lives?

Do we surround ourselves with only those who are just like us, or do we extend ourselves to those who are different from us?

Who are our friends?

Do we make every effort to reach out and build new relationships, so that strangers become our friends?

Is the circle of our friendship growing, or do we have pretty much the same friends that we have had for years?

Hospitality does not just happen. It must be intentional. Inclusion does not just happen. It should be taught, embraced, and lived. And the level of inclusion that Jesus commanded requires self-denial and humility, not just kindness. We must be able to see people with Jesus' eyes.

I must say, I am blessed to be a part of such a diverse church. We have brothers and sisters from all different walks of life. Each has a unique story. We all come together as a family of God to worship Him, but if we are not careful, our inclusion shown through our diversity and unity can be superficial and limited to midweek and Sunday services. Jesus' call for inclusion was far deeper, and the first church understood it:

> *They were continually devoting themselves to the apostles' teaching and to fellowship, to the breaking of bread and to prayer.*
>
> —Acts 2:42

Inspired by the Holy Spirit, when Luke penned what the first church in Jerusalem was like soon after the famous story of the baptism of three thousand believers, he used a very powerful Greek word for "continually devoting," which is προδκαρτερέω (*proskartereo*) from προδ (*pros*) and κρατος (*kratos*), which respectively mean "toward, interactively with" and "prevailing strength." So the literal translation of "continually devoting" would be "continuing to do something with intense effort and strength despite difficulty." Their togetherness had the intense purposes of learning from the apostles, having life-changing fellowship, having common meals where every believer was treated the same, and praying to turn the world upside down!

This was *the* picture of Jesus' unreasonable inclusion.

As the body of Christ, our church should reflect

the heart of Jesus and be completely inclusive, welcoming everyone, regardless of their background. But we also should reflect the purpose behind it, which is to share the gospel. Being kind and welcoming does not mean that we do not hold to the standard of life that God set forth. We are all sinners, so all sinners should be welcome to our church, but we should not welcome the sins. The world is more hostile than ever toward the church. We are regarded as arrogant, biased, closed-minded, and intolerant, so we can be tempted to shrink back and embrace the world's idea of inclusion, which is to accept anything and everything.

But it should not be.

We should uphold Jesus' idea of inclusion, which is to accept every soul but not their sins. We should preach both acceptance and repentance. We bring people into our lives so that they can have a new life in Christ, not just have some place to go midweek and on Sundays. This inclusion means encouraging one another to go deeper into God's word, coming together even when it is inconvenient, eating together at homes with sincere and glad hearts, and *agonizomai*-ing in prayer (Colossians 4:12) for one another.

Jesus' call for inclusion is unreasonable to the world's eye because of its paradoxical principle: We should accept everyone but call them to repent of their sins. To the world, it seems conditional, judgmental, and even harsh. But that is God's nature. He is all loving, yet holy and just. And that is what our inclusion of people should look like, whether the world accepts it or not.

> *First of all, then, I urge that entreaties and prayers, petitions and thanksgivings, be made on behalf of all men, for kings and all who are in authority, so that we may lead a tranquil and quiet life in all godliness and dignity. This is good and acceptable in the sight of God our Savior, who desires all men to be saved and to come to the knowledge of the truth.*
>
> —1 Timothy 2:1–4

God wants everyone to be saved, to have a lasting relationship with Him, so Jesus came, died on the cross once for all, and was resurrected after three days to give us the hope of eternity. God wants to include everyone in His family and opens His arms wide to everyone. *But*—and it is a big one—they must choose Him in response. They must open their arms wide to Him as well, and the only way to be a part of this inclusion is through faith and repentance.

Yes, we should reach out and welcome anyone and everyone into the kingdom of God, however uncomfortable or difficult it may be because of our own background. And at the same time, we should remember the very purpose of this *unreasonable* inclusion: to seek and to save that which was lost.

Chapter Four

Unreasonable Exclusivity

I will begin this chapter by saying this: To the world's eye, this chapter may be the most unreasonable of all the chapters in this book.

Why?

The world wants us to believe that all religions are pretty much the same, and that they all eventually lead to the same spiritual destination. But in this chapter, we are going to talk about Jesus being *the only way* to God.

> *Jesus said to him, "I am the way, and the truth, and the life; no one comes to the Father but through Me."*
>
> —John 14:6

This declaration of Jesus is the most unreasonable

for non-Christians. This is earth-shatteringly problematic in the religious world. That little word "the," which is simply ἡ (*hei*) in Greek, is a definite article, representing the exclusive and definitive nature of a following noun. Jesus was saying that He is the *only* way, truth, and life, not one of many. There is just no way around this hard truth. Peter echoed this unreasonable exclusivity in one of his sermons:

> *Then Peter, filled with the Holy Spirit, said to them, "Rulers and elders of the people, if we are on trial today for a benefit done to a sick man, as to how this man has been made well, let it be known to all of you and to all the people of Israel, that by the name of Jesus Christ the Nazarene, whom you crucified, whom God raised from the dead—by this name this man stands here before you in good health. He is the stone which was rejected by you, the builders, but which became the chief corner stone. And there is salvation in no one else; for there is no other name under heaven that has been given among men by which we must be saved."*
>
> —Acts 4:8–12

Considering his audience, Peter was really asking for trouble by preaching this sermon. But Peter had no choice. He heard what Jesus said about Himself. That is how the truth goes. It is absolute, eternal, fundamental, immutable, inviolable, ultimate, and universal. For Peter, fear could not change the truth. The very next verse describes the reaction to this truth, and it is quite impressive:

> *Now as they observed the confidence of Peter and John and understood that they were uneducated and untrained men, they were amazed, and began to recognize them as having been with Jesus.*
>
> —Acts 4:13

The Jewish rulers and elders could not accept the truth about Jesus, but they saw how it transformed the two lowly fishermen from Galilee into the bold and charismatic evangelists who stood before them. They had no explanation for it, but however unreasonable the message was, they could not deny the power that came from believing in Jesus as the only way, the Son of God. It was plain and real.

So how, then, do we bring this message of unreasonable exclusivity about Jesus to those around us? His word teaches us about it:

> *Sanctify Christ as Lord in your hearts, always being ready to make a defense to everyone who asks you to give an account for the hope that is in you, yet with gentleness and reverence.*
>
> —1 Peter 3:15

There is no way to sugarcoat the truth about Jesus

being the exclusive path to God and heaven. People will disagree, be offended, and oppose. Our goal is not to convince, but to give the reason for our hope in Jesus. We simply provide our answer and leave the rest for the listener to decide. But as the scripture above says, there is a certain way to do this. It is not about what we say but about how we say it, since the "what" is the truth itself. We are to be gentle, not argumentative; and respectful, not condescending, when we talk to others about Jesus. We should remember that they have the God-given freedom to disagree and not accept the exclusivity of Jesus. We can disagree and respect at the same time.

In one of the most famous scriptures, Jesus through John spoke of Himself in this way:

> *"For God so loved the world, that He gave His only begotten Son, that whoever believes in Him shall not perish, but have eternal life."*
>
> —John 3:16

The words "only begotten" in Greek are μονογενής (*monogeneis*) from μόνος (*monos*) and γίνομαι (*ginomai*), which respectively mean "sole or single" and "emerge or become." So the term literally means "solely become or one of a kind." There is no other Son of God than Jesus Himself, period. There is no middle ground for it, and it requires a choice and the acceptance of the consequences.

So being a Christian indeed means forgoing all other religions in the world, however popular they may be. There is no interfaith path that connects Jesus to other religions, as some may propose. God's word does not teach it at all. For most of us, this is an uncomfortable stance that we must take because we prefer that people like us. So we do not take this belief lightly but with sober understanding that God's word trumps everything. We *choose* to believe in God's word, and that gives us *no choice* in proclaiming who Jesus is: the only way, truth, and life.

And this idea of exclusivity goes deeper into our Christianity. Remember this scripture?

> *And someone said to Him, "Lord, are there just a few who are being saved?" And He said to them, "Strive to enter through the narrow door; for many, I tell you, will seek to enter and will not be able."*
>
> —Luke 13:23–24

According to these words of Jesus, even among those who claim to believe in Him, only a few, relatively speaking, will be saved. We do not know the exact number, but it is clearly implied that the number is comparatively very small. Jesus also said:

> *"Not everyone who says to Me, 'Lord, Lord,' will enter the kingdom of heaven, but he who does the will of My Father who is in heaven will enter. Many will say to Me on that day, 'Lord, Lord, did we not prophesy in Your name, and in Your name cast out demons, and in Your name perform many miracles?' And then I will declare to them, 'I never knew you; DEPART FROM ME, YOU WHO PRACTICE LAWLESSNESS.'"*
>
> —Matthew 7:21–23

This almost sounds harsh, but it was meant for those who claim to call Jesus their Lord, not for unbelievers. Again, there is a sense of exclusivity where only those who actually do the will of God will be saved among many so-called believers. Salvation is available for all, but at the same time, salvation is exclusive for those who follow Jesus' word. Although what it means to "strive to enter through the narrow door" or do the will of the Father who is in heaven can be an open theological discussion, at least we all can agree that not everyone who calls Jesus their Lord will be saved at the end. Salvation is indeed exclusive!

Having lived more than three and a half decades as a disciple of Jesus with all the ups and downs that come with it, I know I can become prideful and even conceited that I am one of those who strive to enter through the narrow door and do the will of the heavenly Father—you know, a member of Jesus' exclusive club. And this is where I must realize that this whole thing about exclusivity is not about how special we are as true Christians, but about the urgency of the gospel. The truth is that *only a few* are going to have a true relationship with Jesus and be saved. Hence, how urgent do we need to be, so that as many as possible can hear and learn about this exclusivity, in hope that some of them will decide to strive to do the will of God?

The world is in turmoil as it always has been, and people are looking for answers. For many, they try to find them in their religion. They seek comfort, direction, peace, strength, and, at the end of their searches, the very purpose of life: Why am I here? Some are content with their faith, while others continue to seek. With this broad spiritual backdrop, offering Jesus as *the* answer seems audacious and perhaps even brazen to some. But the simple truth is that Jesus is the only one who offered His life, died, and resurrected for all, proving Himself to be the Son of God.

Yes, we would call that quite *unreasonable* and exclusive.

Chapter Five

Unreasonable Contentment

The topic of contentment is especially challenging for Western Christians. Honestly, we have it too well. Compared to the rest of the world, we all live in abundance. But the irony is that the more we have, the less we are content because either we know what it is like to have something and lose it, or we see others have something that we do not have. We are surrounded by things. Some are essential, while others are superfluous. And we chase after these *things* all day long, wanting, instead of being content. So when we talk about Jesus' teaching of unreasonable contentment, it hits home.

Here's one of His teachings about material treasures:

> *"Do not store up for yourselves treasures on earth, where moth and rust destroy, and where thieves break in and steal. But store up for yourselves treasures in heaven, where neither moth nor rust destroys, and where thieves do not break in or steal; for where your treasure is, there your heart will be also."*
>
> —Matthew 6:19–21

The word "treasure" in Greek is θηδαυρός (*theisauros*), which literally means "a deposit, that is wealth (literally or figuratively), a storehouse, a receptacle of valuables." In fact, it is the root word for both "store up" and "treasures." And interestingly, it is also the root word for the English term "thesaurus," which is "a storehouse of synonyms." So in this teaching, Jesus was emphasizing the point of storing up things.

We can of course store up material things in our homes and financial wealth in our banks and stock markets, but we can also store up thoughts in our hearts and minds, whether they are good or bad. The very concept of storing up means that we accumulate things. They increase in amount. So the question is, what can we accumulate in heaven instead of on earth? One way to approach this question is reframing it by saying, "In what ways can we grow in our Christianity?" Now this is something that we can answer readily.

How about the fruit of the Spirit? These are clearly

defined Christian virtues that we can grow in. And being spiritual fruit, we can certainly store them in our heavenly baskets.

> *But the fruit of the Spirit is love, joy, peace, patience, kindness, goodness, faithfulness, gentleness, self-control; against such things there is no law.*
>
> —Galatians 5:22–23

Who would not want these virtues in their lives? Just imagine growing and being full of love, joy, peace, patience, kindness, goodness, faithfulness, gentleness, and self-control in your life. You would surely be a *small Christ.* But Jesus knew that these spiritual treasures could not be had easily. To have these, one had to give up something else: *oneself.*

In economics, there is a famous principle called opportunity cost. It states: *The opportunity cost of any decision is the value of the next best alternative that was not taken.* In other words, it is what you give up when you make a choice. The big truth in this world is that we cannot have everything. We must make choices. We must give up something to have something else. So we make millions of choices, big and small, all our lives, so that we can build our lives. And contentment is no exception. It requires an opportunity cost.

The question here is not: Are you happy? It is: Are you filled up spiritually? The contentment that Jesus commands is not a feeling but a state of being. It is who you are. And it can only come from deciding to become—of all things—*nothing* (Philippians 2:7) by giving up self. Hence, it is unreasonable.

The world wants us to have things, many things, both tangible and intangible. We are inundated with ad after ad on every possible communication medium, from TV to outdoor billboards to social media. The world wants us to believe that what we have defines who we are and how people will treat us. It is the never-ending cycle of *you can never have enough.* It is like being a billionaire with a mega yacht docked in Monaco just to see a yet bigger yacht passing by. It never ends, not even for someone like Elon Musk. So chasing after material treasures is like "chasing after the wind" (Ecclesiastes 2:11), and these treasures are not treasures at all; the real treasures are within the followers of Jesus in the form of spiritual maturity, because that leads to eternal life.

Materialism is the antithesis of contentment, and the world runs on it. But Jesus warned against it:

> *Someone in the crowd said to Him, "Teacher, tell my brother to divide the family inheritance with me." But He said to him, "Man, who*

appointed Me a judge or arbitrator over you?" Then He said to them, "Beware, and be on your guard against every form of greed; for not even when one has an abundance does his life consist of his possessions." And He told them a parable, saying, "The land of a rich man was very productive. And he began reasoning to himself, saying, 'What shall I do, since I have no place to store my crops?' Then he said, 'This is what I will do: I will tear down my barns and build larger ones, and there I will store all my grain and my goods. And I will say to my soul, "Soul, you have many goods laid up for many years to come; take your ease, eat, drink and be merry."' But God said to him, 'You fool! This very night your soul is required of you; and now who will own what you have prepared?' So is the man who stores up treasure for himself, and is not rich toward God."

—Luke 12:13–21

It is one thing to be called a fool by someone, but it is a whole other thing to be called a fool by God! What was this man's problem? It was not that he was rich, because he only planted; God is the one who gave him the abundant harvest. His strategic thinking of building larger barns was not a sin in and of itself either. It was his selfish desires. He was thinking only about himself, how he would enjoy the wealth. He could only see the blessings, not the Blesser, and even then, he saw them as the results of his own labor, not as God's gift.

As such, materialism blinds people. Greed blinds people. Money itself is not sinful. It is only a tool of trade. But the love of money *is* a sin. It is the root of all kinds of evil, and God wants to save us from those evils through His teaching of unreasonable contentment. The ultimate contentment is not conditional as Paul described it:

> *I know how to get along with humble means, and I also know how to live in prosperity; in any and every circumstance I have learned the secret of being filled and going hungry, both of having abundance and suffering need. I can do all things through Him who strengthens me.*
>
> —Philippians 4:12–13

It is very interesting to note that "I have learned the secret" is actually one Greek word that was used only once in the entire New Testament: μεμύημαι (*memyemai*), which comes from μυστήριον (*mustayrion*), which means "mystery." This word implies entry into an experiential knowledge reserved for the inner person rather than mere intellectual grasp. In other words, the secret of being content cannot be learned only through studying the Bible; one must be willing to experience all kinds of circumstances, so that through them, one eventually learns this mysterious state of being where one is not in want, just like David proclaimed:

> *The LORD is my shepherd,*

I shall not want.

—Psalm 23:1

And both Paul and David clearly acknowledged that this unreasonable contentment is all because of who God is, the perfect Shepherd who provides strength to overcome all circumstances. That is the secret: The source of contentment is God, period. When we focus our hearts and minds on God, contentment is something to be grasped. No self-will or self-discipline can achieve it. It is beyond the realm of humanity. It makes sense because contentment must be heavenly to overcome all earthly desires.

So what does focusing our hearts and minds on God look like? Jesus had the answer for that, too:

> *"For this reason I say to you, do not be worried about your life, as to what you will eat or what you will drink; nor for your body, as to what you will put on. Is not life more than food, and the body more than clothing? Look at the birds of the air, that they do not sow, nor reap nor gather into barns, and yet your heavenly Father feeds them. Are you not worth much more than they? And who of you by being worried can add a single hour to his life? And why are you worried about clothing? Observe how the lilies of the field grow; they do not toil nor do they spin, yet I say to you that not even Solomon in all his glory clothed himself like one of these. But if God so clothes the grass of the field, which is alive today and*

> *tomorrow is thrown into the furnace, will He not much more clothe you? You of little faith! Do not worry then, saying, 'What will we eat?' or 'What will we drink?' or 'What will we wear for clothing?' For the Gentiles eagerly seek all these things; for your heavenly Father knows that you need all these things. But seek first His kingdom and His righteousness, and all these things will be added to you.*
>
> *"So do not worry about tomorrow; for tomorrow will care for itself. Each day has enough trouble of its own."*
>
> —Matthew 6:25–34

This is easier said than done. These are the essentials in our lives, and it is natural for us to worry about them. But even then, Jesus taught people not to do so. Instead, He redirected their focus toward God's kingdom and righteousness. He never promised that He would meet all our wants when we seek Him first, but only our needs. That is the key. When our wants and needs are aligned, we become mature spiritually, able to find contentment within our hearts.

But my little life can attest that we go in and out of the state of contentment all the time, and that is why we must be reminded all the time to seek God's kingdom and righteousness first, that is, above all else in our lives. So what does seeking God's kingdom and His righteousness first mean?

The word "kingdom" is βασιλεία (*basileia*) in Greek,

and yes, it means "kingdom," the realm in which a king sovereignly rules. A kingdom always requires a king and subjects. In God's kingdom, God is obviously the king, and His subjects are us. Since God rules all, both believers and nonbelievers are His subjects. The word "righteousness" is δίκαιοσύνη (*dikaiosunei*) in Greek, and it literally means "judicial approval." So it means God's "judicial approval," hence "what is deemed right by God."

With this understanding, then, we have a better idea about this command of Jesus. What He could be saying is that we should *seek first to worship God, have a relationship with Him, and love people around us in the ways that He deems right.* Yes, we naturally have many concerns and worries in our lives, but at the same time, we should strive (*agonizomai*) to have an intimate relationship with God through our Bible studies and prayers, meaningful fellowship with other Christians, and loving and serving all people around us. Jesus wants us to seek first to *be like Him*, and He will take care of our needs.

We can again look into Paul's words to learn about how we can seek contentment in Jesus in a practical way:

> *Finally, brethren, whatever is true, whatever is honorable, whatever is right, whatever is pure, whatever is lovely, whatever is of good repute,*

if there is any excellence and if anything worthy of praise, dwell on these things. The things you have learned and received and heard and seen in me, practice these things, and the God of peace will be with you.

—Philippians 4:8–9

This is one of the most quoted scriptures, and it is easy to rattle off these descriptions. But when you study them closely, it is much more powerful. Here are the literal meanings of these words:

True: ἀληθής (*alaythayce*), meaning "what cannot be hidden."

Honorable: σεμνός (*semnos*), meaning "to revere, to be in awe."

Right: δίκαιος (*dikaios*), meaning "approved by God."

Pure: ἁγνος (*hagnos*), meaning "holy."

Lovely: προσφιλές (*prosphilays*), meaning "worth the effort to have and embrace."

Of good repute: εὔφημος (*euphaymos*), meaning "well spoken of."

Excellent: ἀρετή (*aretay*), meaning "virtue, valor."

Worthy of praise: ἔπαινος (*epainos*), meaning "fitting of praise, accurate acknowledgment."

Instead of looking for examples for each of these adjectives, if we were to look for one thing that encompasses all these meanings, we arrive at no other place than this: the foot of the cross of Jesus Christ.

Indeed. When we wholeheartedly dwell on the cross, we are genuinely grateful for every single thing in our lives despite difficulties and hardships. And there, we find the state of contentment that is truly unreasonable for the world to comprehend. But we understand it so well, so humbly: God's gift to us was *Himself*, the Perfection, the Ultimate, the Whole, *I AM WHO I AM.*

Being content is a command, not an option, for Jesus' followers. When we understand this, we do not simply find ourselves being content; we actively pursue what it is to be unreasonably content, so that through it, we testify to the power within, fueled by the Holy Spirit Himself, that transforms us to be more like our Lord and Savior whose soul was unshakable and resolute in His purpose. Being content is not the endgame. It is a means to an end: reflecting the heart of Jesus as with a mirror.

Our unreasonable contentment should be a reason for others to question: "How can you be at peace despite what you are going through?" And our answer should be a resounding proclamation: *Jesus the Unreasonable.*

Chapter Six

Unreasonable Judgment

"If your right eye makes you stumble, tear it out and throw it from you; for it is better for you to lose one of the parts of your body, than for your whole body to be thrown into hell. If your right hand makes you stumble, cut it off and throw it from you; for it is better for you to lose one of the parts of your body, than for your whole body to go into hell."

—Matthew 5:29–30

"Do not fear those who kill the body but are unable to kill the soul; but rather fear Him who is able to destroy both soul and body in hell."

—Matthew 10:28

"Woe to you, scribes and Pharisees, hypocrites, because you travel around on sea and land to make one proselyte; and when he becomes one, you make him twice as much a son of hell as yourselves."

—Matthew 23:15

"You serpents, you brood of vipers, how will you escape the sentence of hell?"

—Matthew 23:33

"But I will warn you whom to fear: fear the One who, after He has killed, has authority to cast into hell; yes, I tell you, fear Him!"

—Luke 12:5

Yes, these are Jesus' very own words. Yes, He preached about hell. Yes, He judged people. As the world tries to convince people that Christianity is a feel-good religion, many ministers have indeed shied away from preaching the subjects of hell and judgment altogether. In turn, so-called progressive Christianity has inundated the world with the gospel that only focuses on God's love but not our sins. It is all about just believing God is all love and having this blissful feeling about it, especially through the help of "worshiptainment," without the call to a godly and necessary response of repentance. It is all about how to make Christianity attractive and approachable, rather than proclaiming it as a *soul-saving spiritual war cry.* True, God is—above all else—love, and the cross is about grace, mercy, and redemption, but in the midst of all these palatable theologies, there lies the truth about God's judgment as well. We cannot ignore it or dismiss it just because it is uncomfortable to talk about it.

God is loving, but He is also holy and just. Sin can be forgiven through the blood of the cross, but it cannot be tolerated. Forgiveness is a gift to those who seek humbly, but it is not a spiritual provision for all. The truth about sin is that it must either be forgiven or judged. God does not want to send people to hell. In fact, He wants all people to be saved (1 Timothy 2:3–4). But even His desire to save cannot triumph over people's free will. If one chooses not to seek forgiveness of their sins and is unrepentant about them, those sins remain, and they will eventually be judged. The truth is as simple as that.

> *Truly, truly, I say to you, an hour is coming and now is, when the dead will hear the voice of the Son of God, and those who hear will live. For just as the Father has life in Himself, even so He gave to the Son also to have life in Himself; and He gave Him authority to execute judgment, because He is the Son of Man. Do not marvel at this; for an hour is coming, in which all who are in the tombs will hear His voice, and will come forth; those who did the good deeds to a resurrection of life, those who committed the evil deeds to a resurrection of judgment.*
>
> —John 5:25–29

Judgment Day is not some mere religious concoction

created by Christian leaders to sow fear into believers. It is a divine truth that Jesus Himself preached about, and He is at the center of it all. It is as real as the air itself. *All* will be judged. And for many, this is unreasonable. It literally sounds too judgmental, unloving, graceless, and merciless, as they do not realize that it is a spiritual open-book test. All the answers are in God's word. There will be no trick questions or surprises. He wants everyone to pass the test and live for eternity with Him.

> *If anyone hears My sayings and does not keep them, I do not judge him; for I did not come to judge the world, but to save the world. He who rejects Me and does not receive My sayings, has one who judges him; the word I spoke is what will judge him at the last day.*
>
> —John 12:47–48

To those who *agonizomai* to abide in God's word, Judgment Day will be anything but judgmental. It will be the day of affirmation. It will be the gateway to eternity. But for those who dismiss the Bible for any reason, Judgment Day will be just that. God took thousands of years through many writers to write to us about everything that we need to know to have the right relationship with Him. It all began with the creation that was perfect, but soon, the desire to be like God led to the fall of humankind, which turned the world into an imperfection, causing it to fall under the judgment of God's perfect standard. In a profound way, it was not God but actually humans—us—who brought about the very existence of judgment. So before asking, "Why does God judge us?" we should be asking, "Why do we sin?" If there were no sin, there would be no judgment.

The above scripture also means that we *can* judge one another through God's word. This is the part where many of us are in error. Because we are familiar with the scriptures about not judging one another, we can go to an extreme and neglect the truth that we are to call one another higher with God's word. We cannot be like the world, where turning a blind eye is the norm. As brothers and sisters in Christ, we cannot have an unspoken truce where we do not call out one another's sins. We do not judge people, but we are to judge actions that are sins, in the hope of bringing about repentance. It is indeed uncomfortable to have such a conversation, but it should be done, and with love and gentleness:

> *Brethren, even if anyone is caught in any trespass, you who are spiritual, restore such a one in a spirit of gentleness; each one looking to yourself, so that you too will not be tempted. Bear one another's burdens, and thereby fulfill the law of Christ.*
>
> —Galatians 6:1–2

We all must understand this: Every single one of us is capable of committing the most heinous sin, whatever it may be, before God's eyes. We all have the sinful nature within us. It does not matter how loving, patient, kind, and gentle we are; we all are and will continue to be sinners, needing the grace, mercy, and love of God throughout our lives. And the judgment of God is actually a friendly reminder that the world is sinful, that sin is real, that sin has its spiritual consequences, and that we should live accordingly, pursuing holiness. The irony is that our self-centered human nature seeks justice when we are wronged, but on the other hand, when we ourselves are the wrongdoers, we make excuses and give reasons not to be judged. So we should be grateful that God, who is completely impartial and just, is the one who sits on the throne of judgment and not any of us.

Now about the ultimate justice that is to be rendered on Judgment Day, when we think about it, it is the answer to people's lament: *Life is not fair.* Life is indeed not fair. We all have experienced and witnessed it to one extent or another. Good does not always overcome evil in this world. Actually, it rarely does. Some of the sufferings that we experience or witness do not seem to have any purpose. They are simply and utterly bad. So we lament: Where is this Almighty God? Where is His sovereignty? The truth is that we cannot find this fairness in our lives or in our history because it is yet to come. It is promised in the form of Judgment Day. Every unforgiven sin in the entire history of humankind will be accounted for that day. Nothing will escape the spiritual due diligence and the judgment of God. Every single instance of "That is not fair!" will be examined and judged. The world will become completely fair that day. It will once again become perfect. But until then, God's judgment seems unreasonable. For the faithful, it seems unreasonably absent in this broken world. For the world, it seems unreasonable because of its severity and finality. Jesus nevertheless did not shy away from it but warned about it, a spiritual wakeup call whether one was ready to accept it or not.

Jesus was Love Incarnate, the perfect representation of the wholeness of God's love for His people. At the same time, Jesus ushered in the ultimate judge, His word, to the world. He was both the Savior and the Judge.

> *But thanks be to God, who always leads us in triumph in Christ, and manifests through us the sweet aroma of the knowledge of Him in every place. For we are a fragrance of Christ to God among those who are being saved and among those who are perishing; to the one an aroma from death to death, to the other an aroma from life to life. And*

who is adequate for these things?

—2 Corinthians 2:14–16

According to these words of Paul, Jesus is the same to those who are being saved and those who are perishing, but how He is received is different. For the former, He is the Savior, and for the latter, He is the Judge.

And when we consider the cross, we realize that it was the ultimate convergence of God's love and judgment. On one hand, Jesus' sacrifice of Himself on the cross was the ultimate display of God's unfathomable love for us. On the other hand, God the Father's forsaking of Jesus when He cried out, *"Eli, Eli, lama sabachthani?"* on the cross (Matthew 27:46) was the ultimate judgment of all the sins of humanity, which were put on the shoulders of Jesus.

He made Him who knew no sin to be sin on our behalf, so that we might become the righteousness of God in Him.

—2 Corinthians 5:21

Jesus was judged on the cross for our sins, and He will triumphantly return to judge those who have denied the cross.

So how does God's grand plan for Judgment Day affect my little life? Honestly, it is not like I think about it all day long. I do not spend time imagining what it would be like. Maybe I should. But when I do come across it in my personal Bible studies, I am reminded of God's holiness and sovereignty. It offers the right sense of fear of God, the realization that I am nothing, and He is everything. It also gives me the wisdom of knowing that my life, however infinitesimal it may be in comparison to the world around me, is indeed an essential part of God's magnificent plan, which will culminate in the irrevocable Judgment Day. It gives me hope. It helps me see beyond what we call reality. It motivates me to remember:

> *Set your mind on the things above, not on the things that are on earth.*
>
> — Colossians 3:2

Jesus' teaching about judgment and hell seems *unreasonable* because we would rather reason away our sins. That is who we are. But when we admit our sins, repent of them, get baptized, and receive the Holy Spirit, Judgment Day becomes something completely different.

It will be our Homecoming Day.

Chapter Seven

Unreasonable Faith

I consider the following as one of the most profound definitions of faith:

> *Now faith is the assurance of things hoped for, the conviction of things not seen.*
>
> —Hebrews 11:1

The word "assurance" is ὑπόστασις (*hupostasis*) in Greek, meaning "standing under a guaranteed agreement, title to a promise or property." And the word "conviction" is ἔλεγχος (*elegkos*) in Greek, meaning "to convince with solid, compelling evidence." From this, we can tell immediately that faith is much more than simply believing in something. It literally means standing under the promises of God and being convinced by

His miracles, which can be found in His word. We are the ones who choose to have faith, but God is the one who provides the foundation in the first place. This means that one must learn God's word to have true faith in Him.

> *And without faith it is impossible to please Him, for he who comes to God must believe that He is and that He is a rewarder of those who seek Him.*
>
> —Hebrews 11:6

Just several verses down from the former scripture, this particular one lays down a hard truth, that it is *impossible* to please God without faith in Him, not just unlikely, but impossible. God made it clear that one must choose to seek Him through faith to have a relationship with Him. Faith is not accidental; it is intentional. Yet at the same time, faith is not irrefutable, but it is compelling. Otherwise, it would not be faith at all.

Now with this framework of faith, let's explore Jesus' teaching about faith. Is it unreasonable? We will see.

> *When He had completed all His discourse in the hearing of the people, He went to Capernaum.*
>
> *And a centurion's slave, who was highly regarded by him, was sick and about to die. When he heard about Jesus, he sent some Jewish*

elders asking Him to come and save the life of his slave. When they came to Jesus, they earnestly implored Him, saying, "He is worthy for You to grant this to him; for he loves our nation and it was he who built us our synagogue." Now Jesus started on His way with them; and when He was not far from the house, the centurion sent friends, saying to Him, "Lord, do not trouble Yourself further, for I am not worthy for You to come under my roof; for this reason I did not even consider myself worthy to come to You, but just say the word, and my servant will be healed. For I also am a man placed under authority, with soldiers under me; and I say to this one, 'Go!' and he goes, and to another, 'Come!' and he comes, and to my slave, 'Do this!' and he does it." Now when Jesus heard this, He marveled at him, and turned and said to the crowd that was following Him, "I say to you, not even in Israel have I found such great faith." When those who had been sent returned to the house, they found the slave in good health.

Soon afterwards He went to a city called Nain; and His disciples were going along with Him, accompanied by a large crowd.

—Luke 7:1–11

In this instance, Jesus spotlighted an individual to teach about faith. What is striking is that this Roman centurion may not even have had a spiritual understanding of faith. All he understood was the concept of authority and obedience through his experiences as a soldier, and for some reason, he *believed* that Jesus had the authority to command the sickness that was devouring his slave. Again, it was not a general belief for the sake of believing; it was a belief into something specific, Jesus' authority. Beyond that, the centurion's faith in Jesus was indeed simple, and Jesus was impressed by it, which was rare.

The centurion's faith was demonstrated in two distinct ways. The first was his reverence toward Jesus. As we all know, Israel was under the rule of the Roman Empire, which meant this centurion was the occupier, and he could have commanded Jesus to heal his slave. But instead, he humbled himself to the point where he felt like he was not even worthy to see Jesus. His attitude toward Jesus was like the New Testament version of the holy fear of God that the Israelites had in the Old Testament:

> *But He said, "You cannot see My face, for no man can see Me and live!"*
>
> —Exodus 33:20

The Bible does not explicitly say that he believed Jesus to be the Son of God, but his actions clearly showed his heart and mind about Jesus. No one else in all the Gospels treated Jesus this way in their reverence toward Him! The second was his resolve about Jesus' authority over sicknesses: "Just say the word, and my servant will be healed." His words were definitive. There was no hesitation. He wholeheartedly knew that Jesus' words were the *ultimate command.* What faith!

So a perfect example of faith in Him was displayed in front of people through this foreign soldier, and Jesus did not even have to teach about it but simply acknowledged it with rare praise. People did not just learn what real faith was but witnessed it with their own eyes, and they saw the miraculous result of it.

Jesus marveled at the centurion's faith because it was utterly unreasonable. This nameless Roman soldier apparently had never met Jesus and only heard about Him. It is easy to guess that he probably heard many different opinions about Jesus, both positive and negative, but mostly negative, thanks to the local Jewish leaders who hated Jesus because of His rising popularity among the people. And as an occupying military officer, it would have been a career risk to display such honor and reverence to a traveling Jewish rabbi in the eyes of his soldiers, a hundred of them at that. But something inside him knew that Jesus was no ordinary local teacher. He *believed* Jesus had the divine power to heal the dying. How?

That is how faith works, isn't it?

Here is another famous story about having faith in Jesus:

> *When He had come back to Capernaum several days afterward, it was heard that He was at home. And many were gathered together, so that there was no longer room, not even near the door; and He was speaking the word to them. And they came, bringing to Him a paralytic, carried by four men. Being unable to get to Him because of the crowd, they removed the roof above Him; and when they had dug an opening, they let down the pallet on which the paralytic was lying. And Jesus seeing their faith said to the paralytic, "Son, your sins are forgiven."*
>
> —Mark 2:1–5

Again, for these four men, faith was not some intellectual endeavor; it was manifested into an action. What is interesting here is that their action was totally opposite from the Roman centurion's. While the Roman centurion felt that he could not even see Jesus out of his reverence toward Him, these four men just *had* to see Him, no matter what. In both cases, the focus was Jesus, not circumstances, obstacles, or anything else, but Jesus, period.

Now let's make one thing clear: When you understand the historical facts, these four men's action itself was not that radical, as we may have learned in the past. Houses in ancient Galilee typically had flat roofs with an external staircase. And the roof was supported by wooden beams laid across the stone walls of the house. Over these, people would put a layer of branches or reeds, which was then covered with a thick layer of packed earth or clay. So these four men could have easily climbed the external staircase to the roof with the pallet carrying the paralytic, broken through the packed earth, pulled away the branches underneath to create a hole, and lowered the pallet to Jesus. It was work, definitely inconvenient and destructive at that, but it was not impossible. It was the typical "If there is a will, there is a way."

Besides whether these men's action was radical or not, it is what is behind their action that makes this a story of faith. We do not even know if the paralytic was a friend of theirs. All we know is that they decided to help him, and they knew whom to bring him to, Jesus. Their action may not have been radical, but it was certainly determined and focused. Somehow, they knew that Jesus was the only one with the answer. Does it sound familiar? Yes, the Roman centurion had the same mindset: *Jesus is the only answer.*

At the end of the day, faith is just that. Believing that Jesus is *everything.* He is all powerful, He knows all things, and He is everywhere. And this is utterly unreasonable.

Why?

Our lives are full of troubles. Sometimes we feel

overwhelmed, maybe more times than not. Some days, nothing seems to go right. These are the days when it is all but impossible to embrace the truth that Jesus is the answer. We have to fight hard, mostly through prayers that sound more like silent screams, to keep the faith. But we also know deep down in our hearts that faith is something illusive yet real at the same time.

Another thing about faith is that it is not the absence of doubt but acting in spite of doubt. Having doubt is inevitable, but what we do with it is key.

> *When they came back to the disciples, they saw a large crowd around them, and some scribes arguing with them. Immediately, when the entire crowd saw Him, they were amazed and began running up to greet Him. And He asked them, "What are you discussing with them?" And one of the crowd answered Him, "Teacher, I brought You my son, possessed with a spirit which makes him mute; and whenever it seizes him, it slams him to the ground and he foams at the mouth, and grinds his teeth and stiffens out. I told Your disciples to cast it out, and they could not do it." And He answered them and said, "O unbelieving generation, how long shall I be with you? How long shall I put up with you? Bring him to Me!" They brought the boy to Him. When he saw Him, immediately the spirit threw him into a convulsion, and falling to the ground, he began rolling around and foaming at the mouth. And He asked his father, "How long has this been happening to him?" And he said, "From childhood. It has often thrown him both into the fire and*

> *into the water to destroy him. But if You can do anything, take pity on us and help us!" And Jesus said to him, "'If You can?' All things are possible to him who believes." Immediately the boy's father cried out and said, "I do believe; help my unbelief."*
>
> —Mark 9:14–24

I do believe; help my unbelief. Unbeknownst to him, this man uttered one of the most profound statements of faith of all time. As with love, faith is within the realm of free will. One must choose to believe first. The mind decides, then the heart follows. We choose faith, then God does the miracle of opening our spiritual eyes to see the unseen. Even in the midst of wrestling with doubt, this desperate father decided and declared that he believed. His faith was not that of the Roman centurion or those four men on the roof, but it was real nonetheless. And he knew he needed help in keeping his faith. The desire was there. He took the plunge even when he did not know how deep the water was.

When I look at myself, I have to admit that I relate more to this desperate father than to the Roman centurion or those four men on the roof. Whenever I face a problem in life, my mind can decide to trust God simply based on the truth spelled out in His word, but my heart is another story. The heaviness, the ache, the knot, and sometimes literally the pain that I feel in my heart are so overwhelmingly real that my decision to trust God almost seems like a pretense just because I am supposed to be a Christian. As I mentioned before, at times like that, I recite Psalm 23 repeatedly in the hope that those divine verses will move my heart. It is a spiritual battle, and my faith is at stake. I try to fight off those faithless feelings and pray, but words just do not come out. I feel defeated. And when I do start praying, I feel like it is contrived, words without heart. But somehow God always works it out that by the time I say that last word, "amen," my heart is in a different place, maybe not quite better, but at least getting there. *I do believe; help my unbelief.* Sometimes that is all we can say. And that is what we should do as His children.

Jesus sometimes taught about faith directly, but more often, He taught about faith by being in the moment with those who were quite ordinary and sometimes even marginalized yet somehow believed in who He really was. Maybe He wanted to make a point that faith is faith only when it is lived out. But when He did teach about faith, it was indeed unreasonable:

> *And He said to them, "Because of the littleness of your faith; for truly I say to you, if you have faith the size of a mustard seed, you will say to this mountain, 'Move from here to there,' and it will move; and nothing will be*

impossible to you."

—Matthew 17:20

This was obviously a hyperbolic teaching. Otherwise, we would have witnessed the world map changing all the time! But the depth of this teaching is striking. Although Jesus seemed to talk about the *size* of faith, by taking the example of the smallest Palestinian seed, He was rather nullifying the concept. His teaching was not about the size of faith. It was about either having or not having faith. It was about trusting or not trusting in God. Jesus was teaching this profound truth: The power is in God, not in your faith. Faith is simply a humble and surrendered admission that God is in control, not us. On the surface, this teaching seems unreasonable, but at its core, it makes all the sense in the world because in the end, it is not about us, it is about God, the faithful giver of faith.

So, are we standing under the promises of God and being convinced by the miracles of God spelled out in the Bible? To the world, it is ludicrous and unreasonable to trust a mere book that is thousands of years old for answers to life's most difficult questions. To the world, faith itself is absurd. The world says to have faith in oneself and only trust oneself.

But to Jesus, *unreasonable faith* is the most *reasonable* choice for Christians because they know that they are not of this world, and they serve the Unseen.

Chapter Eight

Unreasonable Truth

Many people say that love is the most important thing in the Bible, but I disagree. I believe truth is the most important thing because truth even defines what love is. Truth is the ultimate standard of all things.

> *Jesus said to him, "I am the way, and the truth, and the life; no one comes to the Father but through Me."*
>
> —John 14:6

Jesus was, is, and always will be the ultimate standard of all things because all things have been created through Him. Truth is immutable. It does not, will not, and cannot change. Jesus is eternal. But because He took the form of a man, this declaration was, yes, unreasonable. To those around Him, it would have been very difficult to believe that this traveling rabbi, probably with worn clothes and dirty feet, was the ultimate standard of the universe. Whatever He said was supposed to be true, however difficult it was to believe. Jesus was supposed to be infallible, *perfect.*

During the time of Jesus, those who defined what truth was were the leaders, such as the Pharisees. They were the teachers of the Law, the theological experts, the political leaders, and the living standard of the Ten Commandments that were honored throughout generations. Their words had the immense influence to move their society. Their version of truth was, above all, legalistic. They knew the Law, so they believed that they knew the truth. For them, the Law was the ultimate truth. So when Jesus, the Living Truth, appeared, it is no wonder sparks started flying, so to speak.

> *The Pharisees and some of the scribes gathered around Him when they had come from Jerusalem, and had seen that some of His disciples were eating their bread with impure hands, that is, unwashed. (For the Pharisees and all the Jews do not eat unless they carefully wash their hands, thus observing the traditions of the elders; and when they come from the market place, they do not eat unless they cleanse themselves; and there are many other things which they have received in order to observe, such as the washing of cups and pitchers and copper pots.) The Pharisees and the scribes asked Him, "Why do Your disciples not*

walk according to the tradition of the elders, but eat their bread with impure hands?" And He said to them, "Rightly did Isaiah prophesy of you hypocrites, as it is written:

'THIS PEOPLE HONORS ME WITH THEIR LIPS,
BUT THEIR HEART IS FAR AWAY FROM ME.
'BUT IN VAIN DO THEY WORSHIP ME,
TEACHING AS DOCTRINES THE PRECEPTS OF MEN.'

Neglecting the commandment of God, you hold to the tradition of men."

He was also saying to them, "You are experts at setting aside the commandment of God in order to keep your tradition. For Moses said, 'Honor your father and your mother'; and, 'He who speaks evil of father or mother, is to be put to death'; but you say, 'If a man says to his father or his mother, whatever I have that would help you is Corban (that is to say, given to God),' you no longer permit him to do anything for his father or his mother; thus invalidating the word of God by your tradition which you have handed down; and you do many things such as that."

—Mark 7:1–13

It is quite striking to note that the Jews at that time did not see the contradiction of the tradition of Corban although it did not make any sense. But all the years of upholding this absurd tradition somehow convinced them to blindly accept it as truth. So when Jesus taught the real truth, the Pharisees were offended (Matthew

15:12). They felt that *their truth* was being attacked. It sounds so familiar, doesn't it?

Even after two thousand years, we still see this battle of truth in our lives in small and big ways. And more so thanks to the proliferation of postmodernism and post-structuralism of the twentieth century. Jean-François Lyotard taught the world that grand, overarching explanations of the world (such as those offered by religion, science, or Marxism) had lost their power. Instead, truth is seen as local, provisional, and fragmented. Michel Foucault proposed that truth is not something discovered but rather something produced by systems of power. That is, what is considered true in a society is determined by its dominant institutions and discourses. Jacques Derrida developed the method of deconstruction, which involves taking apart texts and philosophical concepts to reveal their underlying assumptions and contradictions. This process shows how supposedly stable meanings are actually fluid and dependent on context, further undermining claims to absolute truth. Together, these movements fostered a deep skepticism toward objective reality, portraying it as a social or linguistic construct. In short, people nowadays are "too smart" to believe the truth of God. Some see the Bible as nothing but primitive literature.

With this backdrop, Jesus' teaching about truth is,

more than ever, unreasonable. And a natural response would be: How do we know the truth?

> *So Jesus was saying to those Jews who had believed Him, "If you continue in My word, then you are truly disciples of Mine; and you will know the truth, and the truth will make you free."*
>
> —John 8:31–32

The latter part of this famous scripture—"the truth will make you free," often in its Latin form, *veritas vos liberabit*—is even used as an official motto by top universities, such as Johns Hopkins University and Caltech. Jesus made it clear that the way to know the truth was to *continue in His word.* The Greek word for "to continue" is μένω (*meno*), which means "to abide, dwell, remain, stay; (of a relationship) to exist permanently in, inseparably united (inhere, adhere)." So knowing the truth is not about studying the Bible, it is really about pursuing an intimate relationship with the Bible. It is about living the Word. Jesus could not have made it any clearer: Obedience precedes knowing the truth.

How unreasonable is that? You do not even know whether something is true or not, but you are supposed to trust it and put it into practice, then you will know that it is true. Wait, what? Here is the kicker: The truth about truth is that faith is the key that opens the door to understanding the divine truth. Without faith, one cannot know the truth.

Some will laugh at this as a ridiculous notion. But what we need to remember is this:

> *For the word of the cross is foolishness to those who are perishing, but to us who are being saved it is the power of God. For it is written,*
>
> *"I WILL DESTROY THE WISDOM OF THE WISE,*
>
> *AND THE CLEVERNESS OF THE CLEVER I WILL SET ASIDE."*
>
> *Where is the wise man? Where is the scribe? Where is the debater of this age? Has not God made foolish the wisdom of the world? For since in the wisdom of God the world through its wisdom did not come to know God, God was well-pleased through the foolishness of the message preached to save those who believe. For indeed Jews ask for signs and Greeks search for wisdom; but we preach Christ crucified, to Jews a stumbling block and to Gentiles foolishness, but to those who are the called, both Jews and Greeks, Christ the power of God and the wisdom of God. Because the foolishness of God is wiser than men, and the weakness of God is stronger than men.*
>
> — Corinthians 1:18–25

We were warned two thousand years ago that the truth of God's love will not be accepted by the world but will be ridiculed as something stupid. Indeed, post-modernism and post-structuralism with all their brilliant conjectures would knock down the message of the cross with one simple punch: God cannot die. But the truth is, God did die, but as a human, and was resurrected as God again. It is difficult to accept, but it is as John Calvin said: "The sun is no less bright because blind men do not perceive its light."

Another way to seek truth can be learned from a group of people who were commended by God for their practical approach:

> *The brethren immediately sent Paul and Silas away by night to Berea, and when they arrived, they went into the synagogue of the Jews. Now these were more noble-minded than those in Thessalonica, for they received the word with great eagerness, examining the Scriptures daily to see whether these things were so. Therefore many of them believed, along with a number of prominent Greek women and men.*
>
> —Acts 17:10–12

Before arriving in Berea, Paul and Silas were in the neighboring city of Thessalonica. Their mission work started out promisingly, but then the Thessalonian Jews opposed Paul and Silas' message about Jesus, and they formed a mob and started a riot in the city. So the comparison between the Thessalonian and Berean Jews was apparent. Through the writer of the Book of Acts, Luke, God commended the Berean Jews as noble-minded because of two particular characteristics. One was their eagerness for truth, and the other was their biblical integrity for truth, in this case, based on the Old Testament. Unlike the Thessalonian Jews, who opposed Paul and Silas out of their jealousy toward their rising popularity, the Berean Jews genuinely wanted to hear what they had to say. Moreover, even with the sign of miracles performed by Paul and Silas, which was a customary way for them to prove to people that they were of God, these Berean Jews chose to do their daily biblical due diligence to make sure what Paul and Silas were preaching was true. For these Berean Jews, truth was of the utmost of importance in their lives, and their love for truth eventually bore much spiritual harvest.

We all have our favorite preachers, and it is easy for us to simply trust their words from the pulpit. It is so much more convenient to rely on them to learn about truth than to pore over the Bible ourselves. What we refer to as our quiet times can easily be passive, simply reading the Bible as though reading any other book, instead of going on a spiritual quest to discover the truth of God. And this lack of collective deep biblical understanding and the appeal of consumerist Christianity are leading the modern church in all kinds of different spiritual directions. There are many flavors of churches, claiming many different takes on truth. Charles H. Spurgeon, a prominent English Baptist preacher who was known as the Prince of Preachers, once warned

Christians, "A time will come when instead of shepherds feeding the sheep, the church will have clowns entertaining the goats."

How true is that! All we need to do is get on YouTube. There are plenty of examples of these "clowns" leading their congregations astray, and they are on full display for the world to see.

Truth not only matters, truth is a must.

So how does knowing the truth affect my life as a Christian? Simply put, it motivates me to *agonizomai* in living a life of integrity and honesty, which is such a higher calling for a sinner like me. When I try to live according to the Bible, I realize time and again that I am weak on my own. I cannot do anything good on my own. I am nothing on my own. Integrity and honesty are not part of my DNA. They are the strengths that only come when I am surrendered to the Holy Spirit within me. When I embrace the truth that God is all-seeing, I cannot help but let down all my guards and be as real as I can in His presence. There, I understand my place in His glorious plan, so infinitesimal yet so precious before His eyes. It is paradoxical to my humanistic mind, but it is perfect to His unfathomable wisdom.

The ultimate truth is this: *Jesus died for me.* The entire Bible is summed up in this. And in the presence of this truth, we either break down to pieces, so that

God can make us whole, or we stand defiant, believing that we are good. This is the truth that stood the test of time for more than two thousand years and is still going strong, saving souls all over the world. This is the truth that we, as Christians, are supposed to hold up as our spiritual banner with courage and faith. Once again, Charles H. Spurgeon said it best about the Bible being the ultimate truth: "Defend the Bible? I'd sooner defend a lion. You don't defend the Bible; you open its cage and let it roar."

The truth about Jesus is *unreasonable* because it is not of this world. And we cannot shrink back, because His word is so much more powerful than what the world has to offer. It is the only change agent that can transform someone from within by planting the Holy Spirit within their heart, soul, and mind.

Truth is our offense. With it, we join the battlefield called *life.*

Chapter Nine

Unreasonable Humility

Humility is defined as "the quality or state of being humble. It is a low view of one's own importance; a lack of pride or arrogance." And it can be defined slightly differently depending on the context. Within the secular context, humility is related to intellectual honesty, being able to acknowledge one's own fallibility and biases. It is about being teachable. And in the religious context, humility is the virtue of recognizing one's comparatively insignificant place in relation to a higher power. It is about surrender and reverence. And within the biblical context, Jesus was the perfect representation of humility:

> *Do nothing from selfishness or empty conceit, but with humility of mind regard one another as more important than yourselves; do not merely look out for your own personal interests, but also for the interests*

of others. Have this attitude in yourselves which was also in Christ Jesus, who, although He existed in the form of God, did not regard equality with God a thing to be grasped, but emptied Himself, taking the form of a bond-servant, and being made in the likeness of men. Being found in appearance as a man, He humbled Himself by becoming obedient to the point of death, even death on a cross.

—Philippians 2:3–8

Jesus' humility materialized in two ultimate aspects of His life: He emptied Himself and became nothing, in comparison to who He really was, and He obeyed to the point of death on the cross. His humility was not simply a virtue or an attitude; it was a way of life and eventually death. In true humility, He lived and died. The very unreasonable humility itself.

This scripture is one of the most powerful, if not the most powerful, scriptures about humility. But there is something more to it. I once preached a sermon on this scripture at a house church, and it was titled "The Power of Nothingness." What I realized was that when Jesus emptied Himself to nothing, He overcame all things of this world. Although they were rare moments, there were times when I was able to grasp this concept of nothingness, convincing myself that I did not deserve anything good on my own but only through the grace of God. In those precious moments, I was able to experience the peace that transcended all understanding. Nothing bothered me. If it was something bad, I could accept it as something I deserved. And if it was something good, I praised God for His grace. I felt like I tasted what true humility was like. But, sinner that I am, I could not keep it as a virtue of mine. It is the same with many of us: We constantly wrestle with our pride. Humility is a slippery virtue. When we think we have it in our hands, it slips away. And there we find a familiar face, pride.

On one occasion, Jesus demonstrated humility in human terms so that His disciples might understand it:

> *During supper, the devil having already put into the heart of Judas Iscariot, the son of Simon, to betray Him, Jesus, knowing that the Father had given all things into His hands, and that He had come forth from God and was going back to God, got up from supper, and laid aside His garments; and taking a towel, He girded Himself.*
>
> *Then He poured water into the basin, and began to wash the disciples' feet and to wipe them with the towel with which He was girded. So He came to Simon Peter. He said to Him, "Lord, do You wash my feet?" Jesus answered and said to him, "What I do you do not realize now, but you will understand hereafter." Peter said to Him, "Never shall You wash my feet!" Jesus answered him, "If I do not wash you, you have no part with Me." Simon Peter said to Him, "Lord, then wash not only my feet, but also my hands and my head." Jesus said to him, "He who has bathed*

needs only to wash his feet, but is completely clean; and you are clean, but not all of you." For He knew the one who was betraying Him; for this reason He said, "Not all of you are clean."

So when He had washed their feet, and taken His garments and reclined at the table again, He said to them, "Do you know what I have done to you? You call Me Teacher and Lord; and you are right, for so I am. If I then, the Lord and the Teacher, washed your feet, you also ought to wash one another's feet. For I gave you an example that you also should do as I did to you."

—John 13:2–15

This was in a way a visual parable about humility. Jesus did the unthinkable. God stooped so low, to the level of the lowest ranking slave, to show what can be done in humility. Humility cannot exist in a vacuum. It comes to life in a relationship. It is one's attitude toward the other that shows in words and actions. What is most striking is that Jesus humbled Himself even to His betrayer, the one who would lead Him to death. As He gently washed Judas' feet, what could have gone through His mind? More profoundly, what could have been in Judas' mind as he felt his dirty feet in his Lord's hands?

This washing of feet was also an indirect teaching about servant leadership. Worldly leadership is fueled by power and strength that commands actions, or more accurately, reactions. But Jesus' servant leadership is fueled by meekness and humility that moves hearts. Servant leadership seems counterintuitive at first, looking like weak leadership, but the result is genuine obedience out of free will, which is priceless. It is less concerned about leadership itself and more concerned about the needs of people. And in the middle of it is humility, stooping low to be able to *look up* at the ones you lead, or rather the ones you serve.

Besides the cross, which was still to come, this was the best human example of humility, and Jesus explicitly commanded His disciples to imitate Him. It was a visual reminder that the disciples could never forget because it was not supposed to be. It was a social taboo. It was completely unexpected. It was so *Jesus the Unreasonable.*

When you think about it, pride is found everywhere. If we are honest with ourselves, we will admit that we are all prideful. So it is no surprise that Jesus taught about humility when He witnessed hearts of pride. Remember, He was the best adaptive teacher.

> *And He began speaking a parable to the invited guests when He noticed how they had been picking out the places of honor at the table, saying to them, "When you are invited by someone to a wedding feast, do not take the place of honor, for someone more distinguished than*

you may have been invited by him, and he who invited you both will come and say to you, 'Give your place to this man,' and then in disgrace you proceed to occupy the last place. But when you are invited, go and recline at the last place, so that when the one who has invited you comes, he may say to you, 'Friend, move up higher'; then you will have honor in the sight of all who are at the table with you. For everyone who exalts himself will be humbled, and he who humbles himself will be exalted."

And He also went on to say to the one who had invited Him, "When you give a luncheon or a dinner, do not invite your friends or your brothers or your relatives or rich neighbors, otherwise they may also invite you in return and that will be your repayment. But when you give a reception, invite the poor, the crippled, the lame, the blind, and you will be blessed, since they do not have the means to repay you; for you will be repaid at the resurrection of the righteous."

—Luke 14:7–14

I have never flown First Class, but every time I have had to pass by it to get to my cramped Economy Class seat, there was always someone there who had that look of *I am a VIP*, and practically speaking, it was true, at least for that flight. The seat made a world of difference.

And at this wedding, it was the same. People wanted to take the best seats. What an opportunity for Jesus to teach about humility! And His teaching was rather simple: If you are prideful, you will be humbled; and if you are humble, you will be honored. And He followed up with the teaching about being generous without expecting anything, the humility in generosity.

Times have changed, but people's hearts have not. People still want to take the best seats, be admired, be known, yes, be *someone.* Humility has no place in this world that values self-promotion.

"Being humble is for losers, for those who have nothing to show."

"Show the world how awesome you are."

"Take pride in yourself."

"Fight for your rights."

"You are all you need."

Forget humility, these are the words that ring true to the world. Hence, the challenge for Christians is to stand firm in their faith yet reflect the ultimate humility of Jesus. The world beckons us to become everything for ourselves while Jesus reminds us to become nothing for others.

The fact of life is that there will always be someone better than us. There will always be VIPs, VVIPs, VVVIPs...you get the drift. This means that we all *will* be humbled one way or another, 100 percent guaranteed. Then why not be humble from the get-go? It is logical, but it is unnatural because it requires self-denial on a heart level, constantly attempting to reach down, down, down to that nothingness where the true humility resides.

On one hand, humility should be a spiritual goal for every Christian. But on the other hand, every Christian should also beware of false humility:

> *If you have died with Christ to the elementary principles of the world, why, as if you were living in the world, do you submit yourself to decrees, such as, "Do not handle, do not taste, do not touch!" (which all refer to things destined to perish with use)—in accordance with the commandments and teachings of men? These are matters which have, to be sure, the appearance of wisdom in self-made religion and self-abasement and severe treatment of the body, but are of no value against fleshly indulgence.*
>
> —Colossians 2:20–23

In this scripture, the word "self-abasement" is translated as "false humility" in other versions, such as the Christian Standard Bible (CSB), New International Version (NIV), and New King James Version (NKJV). So yes, one can have humility that is false. But what is it? Paul explained that someone can have the appearance of being spiritual through their religious behaviors, following human rules and teachings, sometimes even to extremes, hence seeming self-denying and humble, but without the true holiness that can only come from the Holy Spirit Himself. Humility for the sake of humility is not humility at all. It is real only when it edifies others. We cannot *try* to be humble. Humility is a product of a spiritual mindset that understands how sinful we are, regardless of how long we have been Christians. A humble person does not realize that they are humble. They just know they are nothing before God's holiness.

I would be the first one to tell you that I was never known for my humility. In fact, I was told more than once that I came across cocky. Being a stereotypical Asian, I was encouraged and pushed to excel in academics, so I did, at least getting my degree in aerospace engineering from the University of Southern California—Fight On! Then, when I got into the full-time ministry at the age of twenty-three, I basked in people's praise of my preaching. One time, an elderly Asian lady even told me that she saw a halo behind my head when I was preaching! So just imagine the size of my pride. It was bigger than my life. I was supposed to follow the example of my Lord and Savior, but my head just kept getting bigger and bigger, as I believed that I would be the first homegrown evangelist for the fastest growing church in the world. Someone had to stop me. And God did.

When pride comes, then comes dishonor,
But with the humble is wisdom.
—Proverbs 11:2

Through many ministerial challenges, I realized that someone with a better heart, a humble heart, should take my place. So I got out of the full-time ministry and never looked back. Sure, I did help people ministerially, but I also hurt God through my pride. When I look back to those days with my 20/20 retrospective vision, I see a man who had a passion for God yet did not understand the true humility that was so needed to live the servant life I was called to.

Here I am now, more than three decades later, at least being able to talk about what true humility is. I do not claim to have taken hold of it, but at least I understand it better. At least, I long for it with my feeble attempts under the grace of God.

The humility that Jesus lived was *unreasonable,* so that we can learn what it is to be growing in our humility all our lives until we see Him face to face. There and then, we will finally know what it is to be truly nothing and all things at the same time, if we can even call it time.

Chapter Ten

Unreasonable Sacrifice

The words "Jesus" and "sacrifice" go hand in hand. We cannot talk about Jesus without talking about the cross, the ultimate sacrifice. But even years before the cross, He taught about unreasonable sacrifice.

> *And He was saying to them all, "If anyone wishes to come after Me, he must deny himself, and take up his cross daily and follow Me. For whoever wishes to save his life will lose it, but whoever loses his life for My sake, he is the one who will save it. For what is a man profited if he gains the whole world, and loses or forfeits himself? For whoever is ashamed of Me and My words, the Son of Man will be ashamed of him when He comes in His glory, and the glory of the Father and of the holy angels."*
>
> —Luke 9:23–26

I wonder how many so-called Christians know that

following Jesus is conditional. A Christian is not simply a believer. They are a practitioner. When we say that we are Christians, it means we deny ourselves and die to ourselves daily. But do we really live like that? Would people around us describe our lives as truly sacrificial? If so, to what point? When Jesus taught about self-denial, it was compared to giving up one's very life. Even if we were to understand this as another hyperbolic teaching of Jesus, it still carries a lot of weight. He is not talking about losing some sleep to come to church on Sunday. Instead, He is talking about real sacrifice that hurts deeply.

> *And He sat down opposite the treasury, and began observing how the people were putting money into the treasury; and many rich people were putting in large sums. A poor widow came and put in two small copper coins, which amount to a cent. Calling His disciples to Him, He said to them, "Truly I say to you, this poor widow put in more than all the contributors to the treasury; for they all put in out of their surplus, but she, out of her poverty, put in all she owned, all she had to live on."*
>
> —Mark 12:41–44

What this poor widow gave was worth κοδράντης (*kodrantes*), which was 1/64 of a denarius, which was the usual wage for a daily laborer. If we were to calculate it based on a \$20/hour wage, it would have been a meager \$2.50. But the Bible says that it was all she had to live on. To her, it was everything, but she was willing to offer it to God as her humble action of sacrifice. The financial pain was great for her, but her gratitude for God was greater. It is interesting how Jesus did not stop her offering. He let it be. The lesson here was too important, so He called His disciples over to teach them. The measure of sacrifice was not how much, but how deep. It was not objective; it was subjective. It was between God and her. No one else but God knew her sacrifice, and that was all that mattered to her.

The cross was the same. To some, it was their victory over a lunatic rabbi, and to others, it was a tragedy. Only God the Father, Jesus, and the Holy Spirit knew the meaning and depth of Jesus' sacrifice on the cross. But this lack of people's understanding about Jesus' sacrifice did not stop Him from going through it, because that is what sacrifice is supposed to be, *selfless.*

I am quite sure you have heard this rhetorical question before: Would Jesus have died on the cross if there were only you in the world? Of course, the answer is yes, and this makes Jesus' sacrifice on the cross unreasonable as well. It was universal yet deeply personal. He died for all, and He died for *you.* His one grand act of sacrifice was enough to bring about salvation for all people and for all time. How? Because He was perfect, so His sacrifice was perfect.

And His sacrifice hurt Him deeply. It was overwhelming even to Jesus:

> *And He came out and proceeded as was His custom to the Mount of Olives; and the disciples also followed Him. When He arrived at the place, He said to them, "Pray that you may not enter into temptation." And He withdrew from them about a stone's throw, and He knelt down and began to pray, saying, "Father, if You are willing, remove this cup from Me; yet not My will, but Yours be done." Now an angel from heaven appeared to Him, strengthening Him. And being in agony He was praying very fervently; and His sweat became like drops of blood, falling down upon the ground. When He rose from prayer, He came to the disciples and found them sleeping from sorrow, and said to them, "Why are you sleeping? Get up and pray that you may not enter into temptation."*
>
> —Luke 22:39–46

Jesus knew all along, even before time existed, about the plan of the cross. He had to come to this world and die on the cross, bearing *all* sin on his shoulders. But even knowing this, Jesus felt overwhelmed and was in agony when He was actually faced with the impending crucifixion. The sacrifice was the ultimate, so the pain was the ultimate. Whether it was metaphoric or factual, Luke spelled out Jesus' sweating blood, giving us a glimpse into the physical and emotional anguish that Jesus was in. Of course, the crucifixion was the cruelest form of public execution and was responsible for a slow, agonizing death. But it was more. It served as a public spectacle of humiliation, torture, and degradation. So yes, the physical and emotional ordeal would have been excruciating. But for Jesus, the spiritual death was even more overwhelming to imagine while He was wrestling in prayer on the Mount of Olives. It was the realm that was unknown even to Him, the Son of God. It was too much for Him to bear. Yet He was triumphant throughout the journey to Golgotha. He was resolute and embraced the kind of sacrifice that He had to make on the cross.

This world is cynical. Yet it still looks up to love as something noble, and sacrifice is the same. We come across story after story about people sacrificing for others in small and big ways. It is most common for people to sacrifice for those they care about and love. There are also those who courageously sacrifice themselves for others out of duty. But no one sacrifices for their enemy. Except Jesus.

And this is where we connect the dots between sacrifice and love. If you paid attention to the table of contents in the beginning of this book, you would perhaps have noticed that I do not have a chapter on love. It is because we cannot talk about love without talking about sacrifice. True love is best manifested as true sacrifice, which embodies commitment and conviction, way beyond those warm fuzzy feelings. Sure, sometimes we love because we feel it deep down in our hearts. But true love loves even when we do not feel like it because it is *right*, and most of all, it honors and glorifies God who made us in His image.

Without sacrifice, there is no love. It does not matter how much people write about it, sing about it, and draw about it, it is only real when we are ready to give it to the fullest without expecting anything in return. And there is only one perfect picture of love: Jesus broken and bleeding on the cross. No, the perfect picture of love is not beautiful. It is tragic, the Son of God dying in place of mere mortals. But this is by design, because it is supposed to break our hearts and lead us to repentance and eternal gratitude.

As Christians, we cannot let the world define what love is. It certainly is not tolerance in the sense of accepting and agreeing to everything. Jesus' sacrifice on the cross made it abundantly clear that sin is utterly sinful. Yes, we are all sinners, but our sins are not trivial. Our sins are not meant to be tolerated. They are to be repented of and forgiven. Jesus' sacrifice beckons our repentance, not simply our admiration and adoration.

Also, love is not from within, but from above. The world says that love is a natural human emotion or a product of chemistry and compatibility. But God's word says that it is a gift from God, modeled by Jesus' sacrifice. Human emotions are relative, but true love is absolute. If love is a product of chemistry and compatibility, it is conditional, but true love is unconditional. The world does not know what true love is. The only one who knows it is the One who gave Himself up for us even when we were against Him in our sins.

Having fully understood the sacrifice of Jesus, Paul urged the Roman Christians:

> *Therefore I urge you, brethren, by the mercies of God, to present your bodies a living and holy sacrifice, acceptable to God, which is your spiritual service of worship. And do not be conformed to this world, but be transformed by the renewing of your mind, so that you may prove what the will of God is, that which is good and acceptable and perfect.*
>
> *For through the grace given to me I say to everyone among you not to think more highly of himself than he ought to think; but to think so as to have sound judgment, as God has allotted to each a measure of faith. For just as we have many members in one body and all the members do not have the same function, so we, who are many, are one body in Christ, and individually members one of another. Since we have gifts that differ according to the grace given to us, each of us is to exercise them accordingly: if prophecy, according to the proportion*

of his faith; if service, in his serving; or he who teaches, in his teaching; or he who exhorts, in his exhortation; he who gives, with liberality; he who leads, with diligence; he who shows mercy, with cheerfulness.

—Romans 12:1–8

It is clear from the context that the word "you" was not singular but plural. It meant the entire church. So when Paul mentioned being a "living and holy sacrifice," it was supposed to be pursued by all Christians collectively. Hence the subsequent teaching about unity among them. His message was plain: The church must be sacrificial, and its sacrifice must be on a completely different level than what the world expects. And to do that, it must renew its mind collectively, thinking and believing differently than the world. The world offers all kinds of experts, and some do garner our respect for their expertise, but no one or no idea should supersede the truth of the Bible. More than ever, we see so-called Christian experts who drop a scripture or two to paint their knowledge to be biblical yet rely mainly on secular academic information for their advice and recommendations. I wonder, is God's word not enough to transform people's hearts and minds? If not, maybe, just maybe, the problem is not God's word but us, our hearts and minds toward His divine word.

To love and sacrifice, something must come beforehand, and it is empathy.

> *Therefore, when Mary came where Jesus was, she saw Him, and fell at His feet, saying to Him, "Lord, if You had been here, my brother would not have died." When Jesus therefore saw her weeping, and the Jews who came with her also weeping, He was deeply moved in spirit and was troubled, and said, "Where have you laid him?" They said to Him, "Lord, come and see." Jesus wept. So the Jews were saying, "See how He loved him!" But some of them said, "Could not this man, who opened the eyes of the blind man, have kept this man also from dying?"*
>
> *So Jesus, again being deeply moved within, came to the tomb. Now it was a cave, and a stone was lying against it.*
>
> —John 11:32–38

This is a part of the famous story about Jesus raising Lazarus from the dead. When Jesus saw Mary and those around her weeping, He was "deeply moved in spirit." And this scene culminates in the shortest verse in the Bible: "Jesus wept."

The word "wept" in Greek is δακρύω (*dakruo*), which means "to shed quiet tears, to weep silently." His weeping was not a display of sorrow for others to see, it was a personal moment because He felt so much inside. What is striking is that Jesus knew that He would raise Lazarus from the dead soon. Mary, Martha, and their family and friends would witness one of his greatest miracles. But even then, Jesus felt deep sorrow in His heart. Why? Because He was *in the moment*. He was with Mary, Martha, and others in their sorrow at that moment. He was not the Son of God or God Almighty in flesh. He was just someone who shared in their sorrow. That is true empathy.

The deeper we can empathize, the deeper we can sacrifice. That is what we learn from this story.

The good thing is that empathy is something we can learn from the Bible and those around us who are empathetic. It is the beginning of learning how to agape love others. And I can tell you that I am learning to be more empathetic and am called higher by those around me daily, especially my family. Before I became a born-again Christian, empathy was a foreign concept to me. For some reason, I grew up thinking that a way to protect myself from others was not to feel in general. The irony, or more like my stupidity, was that I had plenty of feelings, mostly anger and resentment. So when I genuinely met Jesus through Bible studies, I learned that empathy was not some noble virtue that philosophers love to discuss; rather, it is foundational to being a follower of Jesus. And even now, I keep reminding myself that *God's heart breaks eight billion times a day.*

Forgiving every repented sin of every person in the history of humankind is unreasonable. Hence, the sacrifice needed for it was unreasonable, the Son of God dying on the cross. So we remember:

Jesus' *unreasonable* sacrifice is the reason for the hope we have, the hope of eternity, another unreasonable reality.

Chapter Eleven

Unreasonable Hope

People love the concept of hope. Hollywood romanticizes it for its own purpose. Hey, one of the most beloved movies is titled *New Hope*. And hope comes in many shapes and sizes. Sometimes, what is hoped for is something simple yet precious, especially in the case of little ones. But at other times, it is something improbable, but one hopes for it anyway.

It is interesting how the world defines hope: a *feeling* of expectation and *desire* for a certain thing to happen. It is an optimistic state of mind based on a positive outlook on future events. But for Christians, hope is more than a feeling, desire, or state of mind. It is directly related to faith because our ultimate hope is in something that is unseen and not found in this world: *Jesus the Unreasonable.*

> *"For God so loved the world, that He gave His only begotten Son, that whoever believes in Him shall not perish, but have eternal life."*
>
> —John 3:16

This is arguably the most famous scripture in the Bible. Jesus spoke about Himself, but more than that, He spoke about the hope He brings to the world. So, fundamentally, Christians are supposed to be the most hopeful people in the world. But are we? Do we live like we will live for eternity? We worry about the same things that others worry about. We hope in things that others hope in. We rarely talk about heaven and the futility of this world. We live as if this world is all we have, so eager to get and keep more things.

> *Therefore if you have been raised up with Christ, keep seeking the things above, where Christ is, seated at the right hand of God. Set your mind on the things above, not on the things that are on earth.*
>
> —Colossians 3:1–2

Even two thousand years ago, Paul knew that Christians could quickly become worldly. The words "set your mind on" are one word in Greek. It is φρονέω (*phroneo*), which is difficult to translate into English because it combines the visceral and cognitive aspects of thinking. It comes from the root word φρήν (*phren*), which literally means "the diaphragm around the heart." So the truest meaning of "set your mind on" can be "to regulate from within, as inner perspective shows itself in corresponding outward behavior." Simply put, as Christians, we are supposed to be fully convinced by the reality of heaven, so much so that our lives show it. Our hope of heaven is supposed to have a transformative impact on our lives.

So, what is the spiritual path to heaven? It is resurrection. It is the ultimate miracle of Jesus. It is the ultimate proof that there is another life after death. Without resurrection, the cross means nothing. The cross was supposed to be the means to an end—redemption and eternal life. Before raising Lazarus from the dead, Jesus proclaimed about resurrection:

> *Jesus said to her, "I am the resurrection and the life; he who believes in Me will live even if he dies, and everyone who lives and believes in Me will never die. Do you believe this?"*
>
> —John 11:25–26

Jesus *is* the resurrection. Someone else did not raise Him from the dead as with Lazarus. He raised Himself up from the dead. He defeated death Himself. He does not bring the hope of eternity to us. He is the hope itself. So as disciples of Jesus, we follow the Hope Incarnate. This means that our faith in Jesus should equate to our faith in the hope of heaven, and vice versa. And this hope is what should carry us through the toughest challenges in our lives because we understand that those challenges are only temporary compared to eternity in heaven.

> *"Do not let your heart be troubled; believe in God, believe also in Me. In My Father's house are many dwelling places; if it were not so, I would have told you; for I go to prepare a place for you. If I go and prepare a place for you, I will come again and receive you to Myself, that where I am, there you may be also. And you know the way where I am going."*
>
> —John 14:1–4

During the last night before His crucifixion, Jesus comforted and encouraged His disciples with the promise of heaven, describing it as God's house with many dwelling places. Remember, these disciples had been traveling the country with Jesus for the past three years, so the idea of a permanent place to rest would have been a welcoming one even if it were a metaphor. And more than anything, the hope was about being with Jesus forever.

So how does having this hope affect our perspective of life and death? We understand that life is a spiritual preparation, and death is a spiritual transition. The purpose of this life is not to have a happy life. It is to prepare our hearts and minds for what is to come. It is about living a life that follows Jesus' life on earth, so that we can receive the same resurrection that He experienced when He rose from the tomb. It is about walking with the Holy Spirit, so that we will live with God forever. This life means much more when we understand its purpose.

And death? For Christians, it is a spiritual victory. It is a supernatural transition from mortality to immortality. It is not the end of life, and it has no power over our souls:

> *Now I say this, brethren, that flesh and blood cannot inherit the kingdom of God; nor does the perishable inherit the imperishable. Behold, I tell you a mystery; we will not all sleep, but we will all be changed, in a moment, in the twinkling of an eye, at the last trumpet; for the trumpet will sound, and the dead will be raised imperishable, and we will be changed. For this perishable must put on the imperishable, and this mortal must put on immortality. But when this perishable will have put on the imperishable, and this mortal will have put on immortality, then will come about the saying that is written, "Death is swallowed up in victory. O death, where is your victory? O death, where is your sting?" The sting of death is sin, and the power of sin is the law; but thanks be to God, who gives us the victory through our Lord Jesus Christ.*

—1 Corinthians 15:50–57

This is one of the most emotionally charged eschatological scriptures. "Death is swallowed up in victory. O death, where is your victory? O death, where is your sting?" I can almost see Jesus proclaiming this right to the face of Satan. There is power and finality in it. In the end, everything will turn out right for Christians. Death is only the beginning of eternity. Our hope in it is yet to come; but on God's timeline, it has already happened. To God be the glory!

However, our hope is also fragile. Because we live in this world of suffering and despair, it is easy to lose sight of the things above and be engulfed by all the things going on around us near and far. And as they say, when it rains, it pours. We all have experienced those days. Things go from bad to worse as the day progresses, and the last thing on our mind is the hope of heaven. It almost feels like a foreign concept. Even when we wrestle to wrap our heads around it, it almost feels schizophrenic and hypocritical. When reality bites, it is hard to see beyond it. When your physical needs are not met, it is hard to seek spiritual answers.

That is why it is crucial for us to recognize the difference between being naively optimistic and being biblically hopeful. Being optimistic is a humanistic choice, while being hopeful is a choice based on faith. Being optimistic is of course better than being pessimistic, but as Christians, we are supposed to have the right reason for our hope:

> *Who is there to harm you if you prove zealous for what is good? But even if you should suffer for the sake of righteousness, you are blessed. AND DO NOT FEAR THEIR INTIMIDATION, AND DO NOT BE TROUBLED, but sanctify Christ as Lord in your hearts, always being ready to make a defense to everyone who asks you to give an account for the hope that is in you, yet with gentleness and reverence.*
>
> —1 Peter 3:13–15

Peter reminds us that we are supposed to have the answer if someone were to ask, "How can you be so hopeful about the future when the world around us seems to spiral out of control?" The answer of course is Jesus. The future that He promised is not of this world, and that is why we can be hopeful despite the current state of the world. Our hope does not depend on what is going on in the world, but on His word that has been going strong for the past two thousand years. The world changed time and again in those years, but His word remained the same and has had the same eternal effect on those who were willing and yearning to abide in it. Through the darkest times in history, the hope in Jesus was the beacon and sometimes just an ember that would ignite again. So history has proven time and again that the world is indeed lost without hope in Jesus, whether people realized it or not. What goes on in the world is unreasonable, inexplicable, and inexcusable. Hence the hope that Jesus brings has to be unreasonable as well, to triumph over what the world represents.

So how is hope in Jesus so indomitable?

> *For to me, to live is Christ and to die is gain. But if I am to live on in the flesh, this will mean fruitful labor for me; and I do not know which to choose. But I am hard-pressed from both directions, having the desire to depart and be with Christ, for that is very much better; yet to remain on in the flesh is more necessary for your sake. Convinced of this, I know that I will remain and continue with you all for your progress and joy in the faith, so that your proud confidence in me may abound in Christ Jesus through my coming to you again.*
>
> —Philippians 1:21–26

When we look at these words of Paul to the brothers and sisters in Philippi, we get a glimpse of his heart and mind about his hope in Jesus. For him, death was not something to be avoided, but rather, he yearned for it because it would be the best thing to happen to him, the way to be with his Lord and Savior once and for all.

Everything dies and ceases to exist, even the largest stars in the universe. But for Paul, dying was his greatest victory. For a man with an outlook on life like this, there is no fear. Nothing can stop him, not even death. What could anyone do to such a person? Because of his hope in Jesus, though a mere human, he was unbreakable, resilient, and impervious in his spirit. No wonder God used this little old man to turn the world upside down for His glory. Remember, he was responsible for the majority of the messages in the New Testament. He was a voice of God like no other. His impact is felt even to this day. When someone is sold out in the hope of Jesus, they are unstoppable.

Then how do we get to have this amazing hope?

> *"The kingdom of heaven is like a treasure hidden in the field, which a man found and hid again; and from joy over it he goes and sells all that he has and buys that field.*
>
> *"Again, the kingdom of heaven is like a merchant seeking fine pearls, and upon finding one pearl of great value, he went and sold all that he had and bought it."*
>
> —Matthew 13:44–46

There are several theological explanations about the meaning of "the kingdom of heaven" in this scripture, but in the end, whether directly or indirectly, it is about heaven. That much is clear. So a logical inference from these parables would be that there is a price to pay for the hope of heaven, which is one's surrender. This makes sense because hope is something that is beyond our grasp, so to obtain it, we must let go of our own logic and perspective. We must let our hearts and minds travel beyond our reality to reach the hope of heaven. Having hope is a spiritual endeavor of the humble and desperate.

> *And not only this, but we also exult in our tribulations, knowing that tribulation brings about perseverance; and perseverance, proven character; and proven character, hope; and hope does not disappoint, because the love of God has been poured out within our hearts through the Holy Spirit who was given to us.*
>
> —Romans 5:3–5

The humble and desperate understand this divine process of going from suffering to hope. One learns how to persevere only through suffering, and that perseverance builds their character to be godly, and having that godliness enables them to understand what it is to put their hope in God.

Like a phoenix rising out of ashes, true hope rises from suffering. And that is *unreasonable* to many.

Chapter Twelve

Unreasonable Mission

Our family of churches has been known for our mission, and we learned a lot about how to and how not to go about fulfilling it as Christians. To many of us who have spent decades in our churches, the following scripture conjures up quite complex feelings, some good and some bad:

> *The eleven disciples proceeded to Galilee, to the mountain which Jesus had designated. When they saw Him, they worshiped Him; but some were doubtful. And Jesus came up and spoke to them, saying, "All authority has been given to Me in heaven and on earth. Go therefore and make disciples of all the nations, baptizing them in the name of the Father and the Son and the Holy Spirit, teaching them to observe all that I commanded you; and lo, I am with you always, even to the end of the age."*
>
> —Matthew 28:16–20

We have witnessed the gospel being preached in more places and have baptized more people than we ever imagined. But at the same time, we made our share of mistakes in teaching and shepherding people to true maturity in Christ. So here we are with our family of churches going through some serious common spiritual challenges. But when we look out, we see that the modern church as a whole is faced with the same challenges. We are not growing numerically or spiritually. Some may feel otherwise because they are with fellowships that are exceptionally spiritual. That is great. But overall, many would agree with my view of the current state of the church.

From the get-go, Jesus' commission to His disciples to go and make disciples of all the nations was unreasonable. Those who were standing before Him were not the movers and shakers of that time. They did not have any social or political power. They were not influencers. They were a ragtag team of people from different walks of life. They were anything but an evangelistic dream team to win the world for the Lord. But there they were, receiving the Great Commission that would shape world history to come. Utterly unreasonable.

But these men, unschooled and ordinary, went on to preach about Jesus as far as their lives would take them. And all, except John, died for their faith. The traditional accounts say that Peter died on a cross upside down, Paul was beheaded, Andrew was crucified on an X-shaped cross, Thomas was killed with a spear, Philip was crucified, Matthew was killed with a sword, Bartholomew was flayed alive then beheaded, James, son of Alphaeus, was thrown from the temple top and stoned to death, Simon the Zealot was crucified, Matthias was stoned then beheaded, and Jude was killed with an axe. For them, Jesus' mission was worth their very lives. It was that important to them.

How about us? How important is going and making disciples of all the nations to us? For many of us, we have become quite comfortable with our Christianity. We sip on hand-brewed coffee as we read the Bible on a shiny iPad, listening to our favorite worship songs on the latest AirPods. We drive our nice cars ten minutes to where the church meets, enjoy tasty refreshments, casual fellowship, and a brief worship service, all in a comfortably air-conditioned auditorium. Everything is very nice. But in all this, how are we making disciples?

Jesus made it abundantly clear that we are supposed to baptize people. And for baptism, we need to preach repentance:

> *From that time Jesus began to preach and say, "Repent, for the kingdom of heaven is at hand."*
>
> —Matthew 4:17

> *Then He opened their minds to understand the Scriptures, and He said to them, "Thus it is written, that the Christ would suffer and rise again from the dead the third day, and that repentance for forgiveness of sins would be proclaimed in His name to all the nations, beginning from Jerusalem."*
>
> —Luke 24:45–47

> *"Therefore let all the house of Israel know for certain that God has made Him both Lord and Christ—this Jesus whom you crucified."*
>
> *Now when they heard this, they were pierced to the heart, and said to Peter and the rest of the apostles, "Brethren, what shall we do?" Peter said to them, "Repent, and each of you be baptized in the name of Jesus Christ for the forgiveness of your sins; and you will receive the gift of the Holy Spirit. For the promise is for you and your children and for all who are far off, as many as the Lord our God will call to Himself."*
>
> —Acts 2:36–39

Jesus Himself commenced and concluded His ministry with the message of repentance. Peter then emulated Jesus' message when he ushered in the beginning of the church. It cannot be any clearer. Repentance is the center of the gospel, hence our mission. Without the message of repentance, a church cannot truly be a church of Christ. If we are a true church of Christ, sin must be called out as sin, and we must preach repentance, of course with love, gentleness, and patience.

But there is more to making disciples. What follows is harder, and it takes longer, a lifetime. It is teaching—not forcing or manipulating—people to *obey* the Bible. Yes, the fruit of making disciples, the Great Commission of Jesus, is obedience, not simply belief or a deep feeling of connection with God, but obedience, period. We love to fellowship, spend time together, do life together, and try to live as a family of God. But how much time are we spending teaching and learning the Bible, not just for the sake of learning, but so that we can apply it in our lives, obey it, and live it, so that our lives can transform into *small Christs*? Where is the passion to know deeper about God's word, so that it can cut into our hearts? People say that they are tired of the same sermons. They feel like they have heard enough about sin, repentance, and redemption. They would rather have special events where they can have fun. Is God's church just a cleaner version of a social club? Remember, the word "fun" is never in the Bible, but the word "joy" is. Special events in themselves are not wrong, but if those are what the church is known for, instead of its love of God's word, there is no mission.

To many of us, the mission of Jesus is not even a part of our Christianity anymore. Our Christianity has become only a personal spiritual journey. We focus so much on being close to God in a personal way that we forget about being close with one another, which is a biblical way to show the world that we are the disciples of Jesus. The pervasive culture of isolation that is devouring the world has crept into the church, pushing Christians into their own comfortable little corners.

So how do we break this worldly spell of isolation? The Bible offers a practical antidote:

> *Do not neglect to show hospitality to strangers, for by this some have entertained angels without knowing it.*
>
> —Hebrews 13:2

We have already talked about hospitality, which literally means "being a friend to strangers." This is a spiritual way to bring ourselves out of our spiritual cocoons. Reach out, get to know others, open your home. As they say, *Mi casa es su casa!* Meals bond people. Eating together is one of the most powerful universal people connectors. Make it a goal to invite others over for a meal. It is the most practical and effective way to love your neighbor as yourself. It is not what you serve, but the why behind it that is the key: because you care.

Jesus did say, "Go," which means the mission is a movement, even a spiritual revolution. It does not stop as an idea; it moves into action. The mission mindset is what creates the spiritual momentum in a church: people hearing the message of repentance, getting baptized, studying deeply into the Bible, and striving to live accordingly. What a picture of a spiritually healthy church!

We all are being sent to share the gospel. That means all of us are missionaries in God's eyes, whether we feel qualified or not. And each one of us has our own unique story to tell: how Jesus has rescued us from this world. And each one of us has our own unique mission field. We are in someone's life not by coincidence but by God's providence, and He gave us the mission to preach the gospel. We are not responsible for the outcome, but we are responsible for the message.

> *And when I came to you, brethren, I did not come with superiority of speech or of wisdom, proclaiming to you the testimony of God. For I determined to know nothing among you except Jesus Christ, and Him crucified. I was with you in weakness and in fear and in much trembling, and my message and my preaching were not in persuasive words of wisdom, but in demonstration of the Spirit and of power, so that your faith would not rest on the wisdom of men, but on the power of God.*
>
> —1 Corinthians 2:1–5

Did Paul not have superiority of speech or wisdom? He certainly did. But his attitude toward his mission was that of resolve and focus. He did not want to muddle the message of Jesus with his theologies. He made a deliberate determination to preach nothing but Jesus, and even then, only the very essence of Him: that He died for all. He took his mission very seriously, and he knew when to step aside so that God could do His mighty work. He knew that he was only a vessel of the gospel, a bearer of the Good News. He wanted to make sure that people not follow him but Jesus. In our missionary work, which we all have as Christians, we should be careful not to present ourselves as having the answers but to direct people to the Bible. We may have accrued some wisdom through our experiences because of the grace and mercy of God, but our mission should not be muddled by our own perspectives. His word alone matters.

When Jesus sent out the Twelve on their mission, He gave some detailed instructions. And in them, there is this point that is striking:

> *"Behold, I send you out as sheep in the midst of wolves; so be shrewd as serpents and innocent as doves."*
>
> —Matthew 10:16

Jesus did not want his disciples to be naive about what is out there in the world. Instead, He wanted them to outsmart Satan's schemes. The word "shrewd" in Greek is φρόνιμος (*phronimos*), which comes from the root word φρήν (*phren*) that we looked into when we were exploring the definition of the words "set your mind on." So the word "shrewd" basically means "to size things up from the heart, being savvy." Going and making disciples is a tough job. We encounter all kinds of people in all kinds of situations. In the name of being innocent and faithful, we cannot simply accept what people say. We should be savvy enough to see through their lies and deceit to get to the heart of the matter. We should be kind, gentle, and patient, yet tough. We are in the business of saving souls, which means that we must think and act accordingly. The Great Commission of Jesus is serious business. And this we cannot do on our own. It would be naive to think that we can go up against Satan's schemes by ourselves. Remember, he was once a powerful angel known as the Light Bearer. So for our mission for the Lord, we must be prepared:

> *Finally, be strong in the Lord and in the strength of His might. Put on the full armor of God, so that you will be able to stand firm against the schemes of the devil. For our struggle is not against flesh and blood, but against the rulers, against the powers, against the world forces of this darkness, against the spiritual forces of wickedness in the heavenly places. Therefore, take up the full armor of God, so that you will be able*

> *to resist in the evil day, and having done everything, to stand firm. Stand firm therefore, having girded your loins with truth, and having put on the breastplate of righteousness, and having shod your feet with the preparation of the gospel of peace; in addition to all, taking up the shield of faith with which you will be able to extinguish all the flaming arrows of the evil one. And take the helmet of salvation, and the sword of the Spirit, which is the word of God.*
>
> —Ephesians 6:10–17

Somehow, modern Christianity has become averse to the idea of being the Lord's army, but Paul made it clear to the Ephesian Christians that they were in a constant spiritual battle. And we are in a constant spiritual battle that is raging ever more furiously and relentlessly. So taking up the full armor of God is not simply a noble idea, it is a must for those of us who are willing to do the mission of Jesus. All the spiritual elements that Paul mentioned—truth, righteousness, peace, faith, salvation, and God's word—must surround us to protect us when we are on the battlefield called life. We must keep them around us at all times for our sake and for the sake of those who will hear our battle cry of repentance and redemption.

Going and making disciples of all the nations? It is a lifelong mission that we signed up for when we became Christians. But unless we understand how unreasonable it is, it will only be our human efforts and not relying on the power from above.

Jesus gave us the *unreasonable* mission, knowing full well that His unreasonable power is within us.

Afterword

As you may have noticed by now, I have shared a lot of scriptures. It is by design. I wanted God's word to take center stage in this book. I did share my own learning, discoveries, and insights throughout this spiritual journey, but I knew full well that His word is the ultimate answer.

The big sixty is not too far in the distance in my life, and being able to go back and remind myself of who Jesus was, is, and will be is a great blessing. As I get older, I realize more and more that I know less and less. This life is a mystery and unfathomable many times, but what keeps me going is the depth of the Word. It has no bottom. I am convinced, enlightened, and convicted all the time. It makes me feel so small yet so large, so fearful yet so courageous, and so ignorant yet so wise all at the same time. How majestic and marvelous it is!

I hope and pray that this little book at least spurred you on to go deeper into the well of God's mind, exploring what He has in store for you. I also hope that the unreasonableness of Jesus' teachings becomes the motivator, not a hindrance, for you to cling to Him and beg Him to show you *the way*.

I hope to proclaim these words with you on that glorious day:

Jesus the Unreasonable, Jesus the Lord and Savior, to Him and only to Him be the glory and honor! Amen!